THE
HARBOUR VIEW
STORY
CONTINUES

The Harbour View Story Continues
© 2024 Harbourview Cottagers' Association

Cover design: Rebekah Wetmore
        from a drone photograph by John Bohun
Editor: Andrew Wetmore

ISBN: 978-1-998149-43-8
First edition July, 2024

Moose House Publications
2475 Perotte Road
Annapolis County, NS B0S 1A0
moosehousepress.com
info@moosehousepress.com

Moose House Publications recognizes the support of the Province of Nova Scotia. We are pleased to work in partnership with the Department of Communities, Culture and Heritage to develop and promote our cultural resources for all Nova Scotians.

NOVA SCOTIA
NOUVELLE-ÉCOSSE

We live and work in Mi'kma'ki, the ancestral and unceded territory of the Mi'kmaw people. This territory is covered by the "Treaties of Peace and Friendship" which Mi'kmaw and Wolastoqiyik (Maliseet) people first signed with the British Crown in 1725. The treaties did not deal with surrender of lands and resources but in fact recognized Mi'kmaq and Wolastoqiyik (Maliseet) title and established the rules for what was to be an ongoing relationship between nations. We are all Treaty people.

The Harbour View community

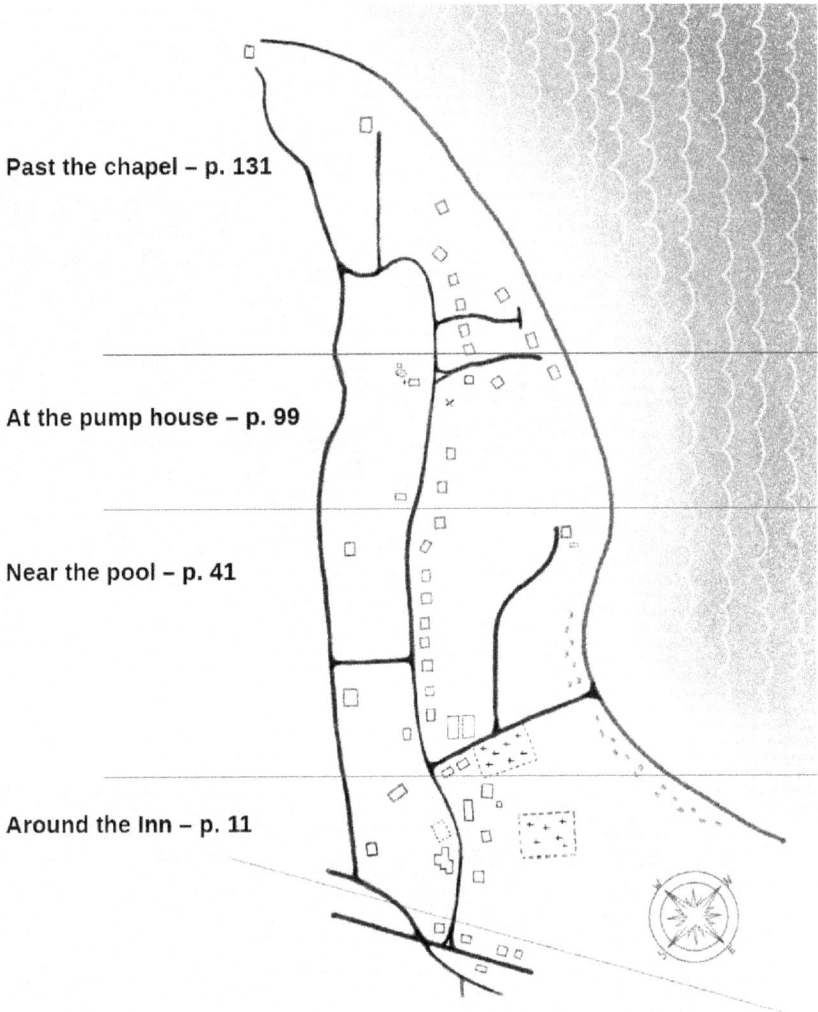

Past the chapel – p. 131

At the pump house – p. 99

Near the pool – p. 41

Around the Inn – p. 11

You can choose swimming, tennis, or just plain sitting.

Introduction

There is a special corner of the world that is situated in eastern Canada, in the Province of Nova Scotia, lying along the Atlantic coastline, in the small hamlet of Smiths Cove. The land itself is gently sloping towards the water, and is comprised of meadow, lawns, a gravel road and forest of both evergreen and deciduous trees. Its viewshed is largely directed towards that quadrant of the sky that runs from the east-northeast to the west-northwest.

As this place extends along the shores of the Annapolis Basin, the vast expanse of salt water—or the vast expanse of mud flats, depending on the tide—also provides a goodly portion of the view.

Upon these acres lie some thirty cottages that fit into the landscape, providing a pleasing and almost timeless aesthetic. Each cottage has its own special character, and a history which is as unique and fascinating as the individuals who inhabit them. In addition, there is a gracious and welcoming inn, a birch chapel, and a recreational area which serves many purposes, including that of a gathering place.

This special corner of the world—comprised of the land, the amenities, the inn, the cottages, and its inhabitants—is known as Harbour View.

There are countless other corners of the world that are very special places as well, but Harbour View holds an exceptional place in the hearts and minds of its devoted inhabitants.

There are many people to credit for this volume being written. First is Charles H. Turnbull, who took it upon himself to write a book entitled *The Harbour View Story* in the mid-1990s to serve as a history of the earlier years of this very special place, where he was virtually a lifelong summer resident.

Another person is Cliff Langin, who suggested that this volume be written to help capture the stories and the history that have transpired since the publication of the original volume.

In the spirit of being inclusive, many other people deserve credit for this book as well. Its creation has been a genuinely collaborative effort, with each cottage's history being written by its owners, family members or former owners. Hence, the list should include everyone who contributed by writing, editing, or providing pictures for this volume.

Special recognition should be given to the committee who helped refine the vision for the book and pull its component pieces together, and to Andrew Wetmore, who, in affiliation with Moose House Publications, oversaw both editing and production.

That there is a community here at all is due to the many people who have participated over the years in making this community the special place that it is: owners, renters, family members, workers, and visitors alike. In that vein, we would be remiss not to mention Sylvia and Dave Irvine, who took custodianship in 1967 upon the transfer of ownership from Walter Flett. Over the years, the Irvines sold off the land and cottages and the community segued from being one with only a few privately-owned cottages to one with solely privately-owned cottages, as it had originally been.

Any Introduction that is too long runs the risk of competing with the contents of the volume. So, with brevity in mind, let us move on to the real story—the continuing story of Harbour View—which follows...

David Turnbull
March, 2024

About the spelling

At various times the name of the village this cottage community is in has been rendered as "Smith's Cove" and "Smiths Cove".

Similarly, the names of the Inn and the main road among the cottages have appeared as "Harbor View, "Harbourview" and "Harbour View".

The official spellings for the village and the road are "Smiths Cove" and "Harbour View", but we have not worried overmuch about consistency in the cottagers' contributions.

The cottagers' association name, as it appears on official documents, is "Harbourview".

Certificate awarded to the first person into the pool each season

To

those who have gone on before;

they are our heritage.

And those who follow;

they are the brilliance of the future.

And to those who show the way:

they are our hope.

The Harbour View Story Continues

Introduction..5
Around the Inn...11
    Harbourview Inn...13
    Winchester House...25
    Birsels'..27
    The barn..30
    The long garage...32
    The piggery..35
    Cossaboom Corner...36
Near the pool...41
    Emberlys'...43
    Langins'...46
    Finally..50
    Courtside Cottage...52
    Eagle's Nest..55
    Linden Cottage...57
    Summerstock...59
    Shady Grove...61
    Lessmore Cottage...65
    Sunnymeade...68
    North Point..72
    New Dawn...77
    Quince Cottage and the boathouse.......................81
    Mountains'...85
    Tall Trees...87
    Honey's Mouse House...91
    Cormore...95
At the pump house..99
Duck Downs...101
    Little Whale Cottage..106
    Wildwood...109
    The Birch Chapel...112
    The Ice House..113
    Boyles'..114
    Birch Bend...118

Harpers'...121
Ballantrae..126
Past the chapel...131
Sea Far..133
Knolltop...135
25 Cottage Lane..138
Seagull Cottage at Loon Landing..140
Meads'...146
Shenstones'..152
Perryford..158
Pillikan...162
Westerly...165
The Cottagers' Association...169
Harbour View Mud Pie...175

Around the Inn

Around the Inn

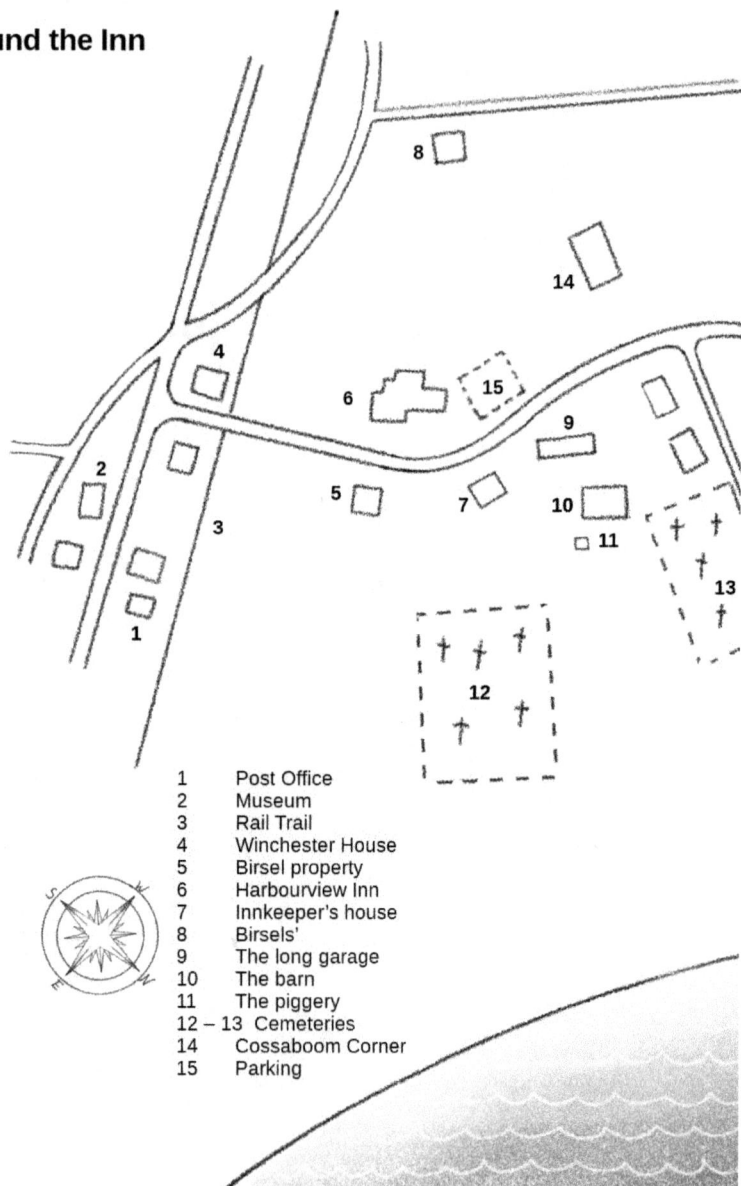

1	Post Office
2	Museum
3	Rail Trail
4	Winchester House
5	Birsel property
6	Harbourview Inn
7	Innkeeper's house
8	Birsels'
9	The long garage
10	The barn
11	The piggery
12 – 13	Cemeteries
14	Cossaboom Corner
15	Parking

Harbourview Inn

25 Harbour View Road

Sylvia and Geoff Irvine in front of the Inn in 1968, before the dining room and verandas were renovated.

There is a certain fascination with inn-keeping that makes other-wise sensible people lose all sense of reason, leave their comfort-able lives, and dive right in. This is what happened, to one degree or another, at four different times between 1967 and 2020 to Dave and Sylvia Irvine, Phil and Mona Webb, Vance Simpson and Darren Snair, and Greg and Belinda Metcalfe.

None of these people had any direct experience in hospitality but all decided to take the plunge and invest their hard-earned or borrowed money to attempt to make a go of it in a wonderful piece of heaven called Harbour View, nestled on the shores of the Anna-polis Basin in Nova Scotia.

The Harbour View Inn has been a place of rest and renewal for visitors to Nova Scotia for over 130 years. The summer resort colony was established by William Cossaboom at the turn of the century and then sold to Walter Flett in 1946, with the present Inn built in 1913. This story will provide a short history of the Harbour View Inn, beginning in 1967, when Dave and Sylvia Irvine purchased the Harbour View House and Cottages, with creative financing that would deter any 30-year-old today.

The purchase included the Inn, 18 cottages, a dance hall, barn, long auto garage, pool, tennis court and 75 acres of land—all for $45,000. Financing was provided by private loans and mortgages held by Walter Flett;. Dr. Fritz Engelhart, a long-time renter, organized the participation of cottage owners, including Mrs. W. W. Turnbull,, Mrs. Rita Mathers, Dr. Allen Shenstone, Mrs. J. Bates and Mr. E. D. Odell; and Dave's father, A. M. Irvine.

The Irvines gave up their suburban professional lives in Ste. Anne de Bellevue, west of Montreal, to follow their adventurous muse to rural Nova Scotia during that spring of the summer of love. They should have known the challenges ahead when a backhoe had to be hired at the end of March to plow the road down to the Inn, where they lived until moving into cottage #14 (now Courtside Cottage), where they spent that first summer with their two-year-old son, Geoff.

Little did they know that it would rain every day that summer and that most Canadians would spend their holidays going to EXPO '67 in Montreal, not visiting a wet summer resort at the western bookend of the Annapolis Valley.

Signalling the family focus that would continue for the next three decades, that first season David's sister Mona Lou came to help with the operation of the business, bringing her sons Peter and Marshall to live in cottage #14 with the Irvines (her husband Philip was attending summer school back in Toronto). All remember the constant row of children's

shoes drying off in front of the fireplace, the only heat source in the cottage during that cold and wet summer.

In the fall of 1967, the Irvines purchased the house across from the Inn from Nell (the daughter of William Cossaboom) and Joe Steadman for $15,000, with monthly payments of $100 and lump-sum payments when possible. It was a kinder, gentler time for buying real estate.

As they settled into Maritime life, it was clear that Harbour View needed new ideas and adjustments to the business model that would improve revenue and manage expenses, which the Irvines thought could be achieved by doing most of the work in-house. Income statements from the Flett period, 1961 to 1965, show management salaries ranging from $2,500 to $4,000 and a business loss of $129.00 in 1965. For a couple with no business training or experience in the tourism sector, their youthful optimism was necessary, as a return on investment took decades to realize.

D A N C E

to the Music of THE TROUBADORS
(with Buster Muise)

at "Harbour View House Casino"

SMITH'S COVE

Every Saturday 9 P.M.

Admission — Single $1.00

Couple $1.50

To manage expenses and in response to how Canadians vacationed at that time, in 1971 the Irvines ceased the practice of cottagers taking their meals in the formal dining room at the Inn, renovating the north wing of the hotel into four motel units.

Many cottagers were unhappy with the change, with long-time summer resident Dr. Allen Shenstone noting in a letter to David during the winter of 1971, "I am very upset by your plan to eliminate the dining room next year. It has always been and still is the place which gave all of us a sense of belonging. We made friends there and kept contacts with our older friends, including the proprietors. Relationships which have existed for the 80 years of the life of Harbour View."

Nonetheless, the decision had been made, with one spin-off being the gradual development of small kitchens in each cottage, which would later make them easier to sell as the business consolidated.

The cottagers were very pleased when a replacement dining area was developed by glassing in the two outdoor porches and reconfiguring the interior of the Inn to make a 50-seat dining room. The second floor of the Inn was renovated during the winter of 1972 to make five modern rooms and a family suite.

Seeing an opportunity to add fun activities and alternative food-service options, the Irvines opened a snack bar called "Shady Grove", managed by Dave's brother, Doug Irvine, in the cottage at 82 Harbour View Road; held lobster boils and hot dog "weenie roasts" on Saturday nights at the pool; and continued the successful Sunday buffet at the Inn, featuring classic dishes like "Lobster Newburg". Geoff Irvine remembers delicious pastries created by pastry chef Josie Rice, who gave him special attention.

CELEBRATE THE HOLIDAY WEEKEND
by enjoying a Maritime

LOBSTER BOIL (held every Sat. evening) $6.00 per person

or

BUFFET DINNER (every Sun. evening)
All You Can Eat for $4.50

For reservation call

harbour view

Smith's Cove, N.S.   Phone 245-4063

For several summers a successful flea market was held in the field across from the Inn and a fleet of bicycles were purchased for rental. Horse and pony rides were always a hit, with many remembering how "Flash" would out of the blue bolt back to the barn, no matter who was on his back.

One of the most brilliant services introduced during this time was the "Children's Program", held in the former Casino (Cossaboom Corner) and later moved to the barn. This program provided childcare programming for children from 9 to 11 in the morning and 6 to 8 pm in the evening, thereby giving parents time to play

16

tennis, ride horses or enjoy a cocktail at the many parties that occurred on a regular basis on the property.

Mona Lou was the first coordinator of the program, followed by Nancy Prescesky, who would marry Doug Irvine, and other members of the family. Many will remember the friendships that developed from the "Childs" that endure to this day.

The Inn in the 1970s

Despite these changes and aggressively marketing Harbour View in national and regional newspapers and with direct mail campaigns, and doing as much of the work that they could themselves, the Irvines struggled to make the business work. Given that the season was essentially ten weeks during those years (an extension by two weeks from the Flett and Cossaboom years), it continued to be a challenge to make money. In 1975 they attempted to sell shares to the existing cottage owners and received limited interest.

Determined to make it work, Dave took on employment in the off-season and, in 1976, decided to renovate the Casino into seven fully-insulated, year-round efficiency units that could be rented by the month in the winter and by the day or week in the summer.

Cossaboom Corner became a reality and provided steady revenue as the Irvines changed the property to year-round occupancy.

Since the first summer in 1967, the Irvines had enjoyed the support of Dave's sister Mona Lou, brother-in-law Phil and their children, who would come from Toronto to help run the business. The Webb children, Marshall, Peter and Andrea, became fast friends with their Irvine cousins, Geoff and Jenny. Brother Doug Irvine also came from Ontario every summer to work for his brother, eventually married summer resident Nancy Prescesky, and built a beautiful year-round home, Duck Downs, at Harbour View with their children Dylan and Nataleah.

For the Webbs and the Irvines, the business was a family affair throughout the 33 years that they collectively managed the Inn and, overall, Harbour View's business. All their children worked in the business.

The Webb's oldest son, Marshall, spent considerable time at Harbour View over the years, initially looking after the vegetable garden beside the Irvine house and later developing a wheel-shaped garden behind the shuffleboard courts and closer to the restaurant. Marsh was a charismatic waiter who managed multiple tables with an efficient flair, and was referenced in the annual *Where to Eat in Canada* guide as being "erratic but charming".

Peter and Andrea Webb both worked in the dining room and did other duties during their summer holidays through high school and university. Geoff and Jenny Irvine spent many summers working in the Cove Restaurant. Geoff worked on the front desk, cut the grass, cleaned the pool, washed dishes and worked as a waiter.

Sylvia Irvine managed the squad of housekeeping staff who, in the 1970s, operated a laundry in the building behind the Inn that eventually was moved down to the shore to become the Irvines' boathouse. Many will remember seeing the housekeepers pushing their carts up and down the property as they looked after "go's" and "stay's".

Mona was the Chef and Phil operated the bar and front desk. Dave managed the overall business and quickly developed skills in plumbing, renovations and carpentry, landscaping, pool care and duck and geese feeding.

By 1980, the Irvines and Webbs developed a plan that would change how the business of Harbour View operated. The Irvines split the cottages and Cossaboom Corner from the Inn and added a general store beside the Inn, "Aunt Minerva's Store", a nod to a former general store in Smith's Cove, to sell groceries and handle front desk duties. The Webbs purchased the Inn and would continue to operate it for the next 20 years.

Dave and Sylvia were proud to report that they had improved occupancy from 35% in 1967 to 97% when they sold in 1980.

Welcome to Harbourview Inn

Dinner served leisurely 5:30 pm - 9:30

Appetizers

Harbourview Chowder
Nova Scotia Fish Chowder.
$3.25

Soup of the Day
$2.35

Solomon Gundy
Pickled Herring with
Sour Cream Dill Sauce
$3.50

Gazpacho
Refreshing Cold Soup
$3.25

Antipasto
Zesty Concoction with
Olives, Tuna, Vegetables
$3.50

Garden Salad
Fresh Local Greens with a
Choice of Homemade Dressings
$3.50

Pate
Mushroom and Cheese Pate with Apple Chutney.
$3.50

Fruit Juice
$1.00

Entrees

Sauteed Chicken a la Bourguignonne
· Sauteed breast of chicken finished with a rich red wine sauce. $12.95

Boneless New York Steak
· Prime quality cut sirloin served with green peppercorn, horseradish cognac sauce. $13.95

Catch of the Day
· Pan fried and served with a lemon chive butter. $11.95

Digby Scallops
· Fresh Digby scallops sauteed with sweet garlic. $13.50

Desserts

Mud Pie
$3.25

Cheesecake
$3.75

Ice Cream
$2.25

Fresh Fruit
$2.50

Dessert Special
$3.95

Cheese Plate
$3.75

Tea or Coffee
$0.85

Iced Tea or Milk
$1.00

In the early years, while Phil was still teaching in Toronto, Mona would load up the station wagon at the end of June with the kids and move to Nova Scotia for the summer. For many years they lived in a cottage in the backyard of the Irvines' home, across from the Inn. Later, that cottage was split in two, placed on skids, and moved down the field and across the beach to become "Quince Cottage", the Irvines' retirement home on the Annapolis Basin. The Webbs eventually renovated the third floor of the inn for their accommodations and lived there for many happy years.

Given Mona's significant skills in the kitchen and Phil's front-of-house acumen, the "Cove Restaurant" became one of the finest restaurants in Southwest Nova Scotia. The menu was simple, with delicious renditions of local favourites such as sauteed scallops, antipasto and, of course, mud pie.

All Webb and Irvine children of the day learned to serve, make drinks, assemble desserts, wash dishes and participate in the wonderful summer life at Harbour View under Mona and Phil's watchful eye. There are fond memories of busy evenings serving cottagers, Inn guests and people from the local area, with the entire family pitching in with Steely Dan's classic albums "Aja" and "Gaucho" on constant play mode (often over and over again each night).

Over the years, Phil spent hours stripping layers of paint from the trim inside the hotel and made many alterations to the flow of the front desk, dining room and kitchen. He dreamed of renovating the basement to make a unique, country-style pub, but there was never enough money at the end of the year to make it a reality.

As the millennium approached, it was clear that Mona and Phil were ready to retire from the business of inn-keeping, so they put the Inn up for sale.

Looking for a change after careers in customer service in retail and the airline industry, Darren Snair and Vance Simpson bought the inn from the Webbs and closed the purchase on January 20, 2000, after a month's delay (perhaps due to Y2K fears). Similarly to the Webbs, Darren and Vance operated the inn for twenty years and had their share of ups and downs during that time.

Darren had worked for many years at Eaton's department store in Halifax and Vance had worked at Air Canada. Both had won top awards for customer service and believed to their core that guest service is about caring for people, something they had both learned at a young age.

Vance grew up in Murray Harbour, a small farming community in New Brunswick, and went to a one room schoolhouse with 20 students and a wonderful teacher. It was at that school that he learned the golden rule of human relations—treat others as you would like to be treated. Darren grew up in Boutilier's Point, Nova Scotia, a small fishing community, with a mother who taught him the importance of strength of character and a father who invested in him the value of hard work.

It was clearly fate that would lead Darren and Vance back to living by the ocean, working hard, and providing a quiet haven for their guests.

Eaton's went out of business in 1999 and Darren found himself at a career watershed. By that time, Vance had worked at Air Canada for 28 years and was also looking for a change. Both fondly recalled their childhood in rural Atlantic Canada, discovered the Harbourview Inn (the Webbs had changed the name from Harbour View to Harbourview, a controversy to this day) and decided to take a chance and buy it.

Vance's handyman skills were an incredibly valuable asset in repairing and updating the hundred-year-old Inn and the even-older Winchester House. As they had never operated a business like this, they hired as many of the previous staff as possible so that they could teach them how the business operated.

It was a challenge operating two businesses, the inn and the dining room/bar, at the same time. Changes to the operation were made slowly but, by the third year of ownership, they decided to close the unprofitable and difficult dining room and focus their energy on running the inn and improving their marketing activities.

By the time they sold the Inn in 2020, occupancy rates in peak months were usually 97% to 99% and they had received a number of travel industry awards. Darren's ability to network and develop new markets was key to achieving these results. They were blessed with an excellent product to sell and had dedicated housekeepers and breakfast servers who took great pride in the quality of their work.

Over their time in Smith's Cove, Vance and Darren bought a home close by and, in preparation for retirement, purchased a lovely house overlooking Digby Gut on the Lighthouse Road.

Belinda and Greg Metcalfe bought the Inn in January 2020, just in time for business to be dramatically impacted by the COVID-19 pandemic. The Metcalfes would happily have exchanged their challenges in 2020 for the wet and cold summer of 1967.

They fondly remember spending considerable time with Darren and Vance in January and February as they learned the fundamentals of the business, and were excited as bookings were rolling in daily, presaging a busy season ahead.

We all know what happened next. The pandemic hit, travel was dramatically impacted, and lockdowns were imposed. They spent March processing cancellation after cancellation. By mid-May, when the Inn typically would be opening, they did not have a single booking left for the year. Greg and Belinda could not believe what was happening.

Faced with a disastrous year, they had tough decisions to make. Their three staff members, Veronica Norris, Irene Evans and Hannah Cosman, had been with the business for many years and were highly recommended by Vance and Darren. But with no visitors booked, what would they do?

Unsure how long the pandemic would last, Greg and Belinda decided to keep all staff on and take advantage of the business lull to spend time renovating the inn.

This turned out to be a wise decision for everyone, as they formed an effective renovation team and had lots of fun working together. There was plenty of banter about decorative choices. During the early part of the 2020 season, the demo team stripped and renovated several of the guest rooms and kept busy focusing on the future.

In 2021 it looked like summer business would still be challenging. Hannah went away to school, and new team member Lisa Amero pitched in. Given the predicted summer occupancy, they stayed positive and focused on more renovations and improvements.

During this time, they took on some bigger projects as well, including building a large fire escape, as instructed by the local building & fire inspector. They completely renovated the third-floor apartment and added it to the rental pool. They stripped and replaced the ceiling in the lobby and reception area, introducing new lighting at the same time. Seizing on the good Wi-fi availability, they modernized arrival and check-in procedures.

Today almost all the rooms have been completely renovated, boasting new paint, linen and furniture. When business recovered in 2022 and 2023, Greg and Belinda had a cohesive team who had weathered the stress of the pandemic and were ready for the return of visitors to Harbour View.

While Dave and Sylvia used direct mail and newspapers for their promotion and marketing (Geoff remembers winter nights printing letters on the old Gestetner machine and licking stamps), Mona and Phil relied on word of mouth and a popular restaurant to keep business flowing. Darren and Vance embraced the internet to reach out and appeal to international travellers, and Greg and Belinda were the first to embrace social media. They now have active accounts on Facebook and Instagram, which have become critical to visitor engagement and bookings.

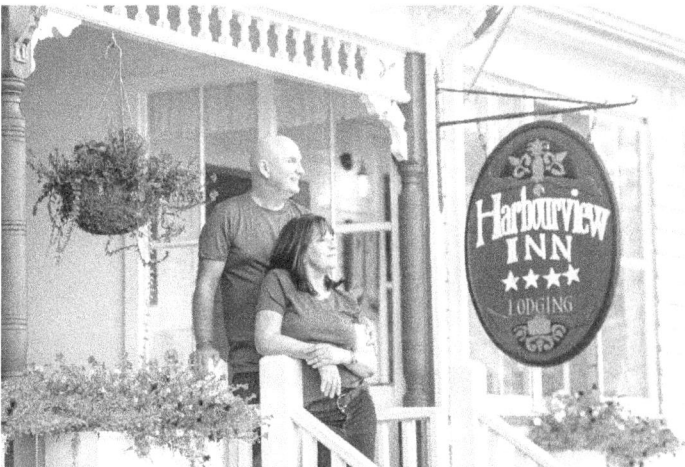

The Metcalfs greet returning summer guests

Like those before them, Greg and Belinda did not grow up in Smith's Cove and came "from away". They have lived and worked in South Africa, Uganda, Ghana and Kenya, and made the move to Canada in 2017. Settling into life in Nova Scotia, they have built a new house on the property, across from the Inn and overlooking the Annapolis Basin.

These families all have one thing in common: they have all found a way to combine the challenging lifestyle of an innkeeper with living in one of the most beautiful places in Canada.

Winchester House

573 Highway 1

During the Flett years and in the early Irvine years, there was a large, inverted L-shaped steel standard across the road from the entrance to Harbour View, on which a wooden sign, about 5'x 3', hung very close to the edge of the highway and was lighted at night by two goose-neck lights with green enamelled shades. The location of Harbour View House and Cottages was indicated by a big black arrow along the bottom of the sign. Power was supplied by overhead wires from the two or three street lights that ran up to the highway from the Inn and were activated by a switch on the front veranda.

After a number of years the Highway Department advised the Irvines that the sign was contravening regulations, so it had to be moved to the head of Harbour View Road.

Prior to that move, it was necessary to widen the mouth of the road to allow for entrance and exit from either direction of Highway 1. Since the Irvines only owned the existing, narrow, right of way, they purchased the building now known as Winchester House, on the Digby side of the road and rented it for a few years, during which they widened the entry way.

The widened entrance allowed enough room between the two lanes for a sign with the updated logo and, later, with a planter base.

Andrew and Rebekah Wetmore rented Winchester House for a few months in 1974 and report that the daily excitement for them (and panic for their cats) was the passage of Dominion Atlantic Railway trains, horns blaring and bells clanging, mere yards from their kitchen.

The Irvines sold the property to Henry and Caroline Saulnier. It passed through several owners, and eventually to Darren Snair and Vance Simpson, who extensively renovated Winchester House to serve as an annex to the Inn.

In 2020, ownership of the Harbourview property changed to Belinda and Greg Metcalfe. They eventually sold Winchester House to Emma Lundgren, who has made substantial upgrades and expansions to the building and property.

Birsels'

89 North Old Post Road

The Birsel family's introduction to Harbour View came in the summer of 1968, when Dr. Nuri Birsel made a house call to a sick guest staying in one of the cottages. He was enchanted and went home to tell Olive and the children in Digby that he had discovered a wonderful place.

The family soon visited for swimming and quickly fell in love with Harbour View. Olive, Nuri and the children—Sezen (Sandy), Marcus, Robert and Kate—became regular visitors.

After a couple of years of renting for summer holidays the family bought cottage #17 (now Summerstock) in the early 1970s.

The family at Cottage 17 in the 1970s: l-r, standing: Kate, Marcus, Robert, Sezen, Nuri. Sitting: Olive and her aunt, Veronic Watrous, known to the family as Arty.

Harbour View at the time was full of children and teenagers, both regular visitors with their own cottages and guests. The Birsels made life-long friends with many of them, including the Presceskys and Shenstones.

People from the community were also an important part of Harbour View life at the time, with youngsters from Smith's Cove working at the Inn; in the stables, where Harbour View kept five horses and ponies; and, of course, mowing the lawns.

One summer, Olive arranged riding lessons for the children in the field by the pool. The very young ones attended a daily "children's programme" in Cossaboom Corner, which was then known as the Casino. Weekend dances were also held there.

A pony and people at the pool

A happy gaggle of youngsters was always around, by the pool on hot afternoons and down on the beach for parties in the evenings. Occasionally, the kids would pile into small boats and cross over to Bear Island for overnight beach parties.

The Birsels sold their cottage to the Hopgood family in the early 1980s but, despite no longer having a place there, the family still owned land on the property and maintained links with the Harbour View community.

The Birsels returned to Harbour View in 2007, when Olive bought the house behind the hotel, at 89 North Old Post Road, where the family, particularly grandchildren Emma, Alex and Julia, have spent many happy summers. The small swimming pool at the back of the house has been a favourite escape both children and grown-ups on hot days when they have been too lazy to head down to "the big pool."

In the small pool, with the Inn in the background.

Olive was a passionate gardener and planted flower beds and trees around the property, which the family has worked to maintain after she died in 2016.

The family also bought 22 Harbour View Road, opposite the Inn, and rents it out.

Harbour View remains close to the heart of all members of the Birsel family, who try to get back for summer visits as often as they can.

The barn

The Irvines used the barn, which came with the Harbour View property, to house cows and horses. The horses played a significant part in the children's programs over the years.

When the Langins purchased the barn, they turned it into a recreation space, with a pool table, shuffleboard, ping pong table and dart board; it is a great place to wile away a rainy afternoon.

The barn also hosts the annual meetings of the Cottagers' Association, like this one in 2024:

The long garage

In *The Harbour View Story*, Charles Turnbull mentions the long, eight-bay garage, that he claims was originally much longer, that housed cottage owners and guests' automobiles, many of which were chauffeured by local chaps while their owners were in residence.

In the Irvine years it housed the tractor, various farm vehicles and implements, a five-hundred-gallon gas tank, and Fred Misick's Hillman along with a few bays of storage.

Included in the storage items was the hand-cranked printing press that would have printed the menus that Charles refers to as being provided new each day in the original Harbour View House. The Irvines donated the press to the Smith's Cove Museum.

The Hon. Fred C. M. C. P. Misick was a member of the Bermudian

Parliament and was a guest in what is now the Boyles' cottage for many summers, until his death in 1976 at age 85. He and his wife, Margaret, owned a right-hand-drive Hillman Minx, which they had shipped from Bermuda to drive while in Nova Scotia.

In the off-season it was stored in rented space in one of the bays of the long garage, until Fred passed away and his son John sold it to David Irvine for $500.

Douglas Irvine enjoyed driving it for at least one summer, after which it was sold to Ralph Fiske, a collector and former owner of the Dresden Arms in Halifax, for $1000.

Douglas Irvine at the wheel of the Hillman Minx

It seems Fred Misick founded the Bermuda Bridge Club in 1932, and Charles refers to the Misicks' marathon bridge games in Cottage 40. During one such afternoon affair David Irvine was a "fly on the wall"—actually "the plumber in the kitchen", installing a new element in the hot water tank while the bridge game, progressed in the living room.

David was treated to Fred's intensity in bridge when Margaret offered a plate of cookies to their guests and Fred's comment was, "Did you come here to play bridge or eat?"

By 2001 the long garage was deteriorating. Prior to the Irvines selling the barn and the land around it to the Langins and Emberlys, they had the long garage torn down. Beautiful wide planks and all of the roof trusses were salvaged and repurposed in building two outbuildings for Quince Cottage: a very solid wood shed, and a garden shed at the back of the parking area.

The piggery

The piggery was located behind the barn, and was still in use in the first year the Irvines owned Harbour View.

One late afternoon, after the hired men had left for the day, the pigs escaped through the fence around their enclosure just as Dr. Doug Black, long-time, beloved doctor in Digby, was arriving to make a house call.

When David met him at the front door of the Inn, where the Irvines lived before their move to cottage 14, the doctor asked who owned the six pigs that were headed down the railway track.

As David shot out the door in pursuit, he asked Doug how one calls pigs.

Doug replied, "Here piggy, piggy."

David ran down the tracks, shouting as he had been instructed, and was amazed to see the pigs turn around. They followed him back to the pen.

Unfortunately, the break in the fence was still there, so the pigs went in the gate and right back out again. They cavorted at liberty until David had a chance to do some quick repairs and then shepherd them back in yet again.

After those pigs met their maker later that summer, the piggery, cleaned up and freshly painted, became the Irvines' garden shed.

Cossaboom Corner

45 Harbour View Road

Original Harbour View Dance Casino, pre-1931

The building now known as Cossaboom Corner has been in transition for almost 100 years. In fact, there have been two different buildings on the same site. The original Harbour View Dance Casino, seen above, burned to the ground in the late 1940s.

Then-owner Walter Flett built the second building in the early 1950s. It continued to be used as a dance hall through the early Irvine years, with music by the Troubadors (Barry Cummings on the trumpet, Puss Peters on piano and Buster Muise on vocals). When the music of the Beatles hit in the late 1960s, the Hall featured a group from Digby, the Purple Candle Secrets, who were given permission to repaint the inside of the Hall in psychedelic colours and use strobe lights to highlight the frenetic action. The dance on Saturday nights drew 300 screaming teenagers, with another 150 on Wednesday evenings.

But success was the downfall, as the crowds interfered with the enjoyment of summer guests, and the dances were terminated.

For the next few years the hall housed the children's' program, dried laundry on rainy days and became a storage catch-all.

In 1977, after a major renovation, including the addition of a fully functional basement, the building held

Wild art on the walls

seven housekeeping units for summer use by guest families at Harbour View. Their close proximity to the pool and playground made them a very attractive alternative to the Inn.

At the official opening of Cossaboom Corner, named after William Cossaboom, the founder of Harbour View, his daughter, Nell Steadman, cut the ribbon held by seven-year-olds Jennifer Irvine and Andrea Webb.

Into the early 1990s, the units were successfully repurposed into long term rental apartments.

By 1999 Geoff and Kelly Irvine, with Will (1994) and Julia (1990) [Georgia arrived in 2001]; and Jenny and Rob Begrand, Oliver (1998) and Ben (1999) were families in their own right and the five upper units were renovated into two large apartments, with central storage and a playroom in the middle, plus a large front deck at the front of each.

In the lower level the former laundromat was closed and became Geoff's summer office until 2003.

In 2001 the driveway was extended around the building and shingling of building was begun in stages, to be finished by Marshall Webb a few years later.

In 2009 Sylvia and Dave began a major renovation of the Geoff Irvine side of the building in preparation for selling Quince Cottage in 2010. The addition of a large sunroom and entrance hall at the front, and a tower that David had always wanted at the back, put the final touches on ensuring the building no longer looked like the

"Harbour View Dance Casino".

Extensive alteration of the interior created an attractively-appointed, open-concept, cathedral-ceilinged apartment for the Irvines. The wood stove from the Quince Cottage dining room, with mantle and hearth, became a focal point in the new surroundings that offered a popular setting for family reunions and social gatherings.

With some minor alterations the other half of the building continued to be occupied full-time by Jenny Begrand. David continued to have his office and workshop in the lower area, along with his tractor and various vehicles in the garage, that was shared with Sylvia's garden/potting corner.

Outside, Sylvia's gardening talent came into play once again, with flowers and bushes adorning a number of garden areas around three sides of the building.

The parking lot across the driveway was expanded and, next to it, a large fieldstone fire pit surrounded by colourful Adirondack chairs attracted cottagers to join the evening social gatherings. A storage/equipment shed was added at the back of the building and a quaint firewood storage building, handy to the wood stove, at the front.

The two downstairs units served various purposes after 1999 until 2019, when Jenny carried out a major renovation to create one luxurious apartment that she offered as an Airbnb until the building was sold to Mali and Amir in 2021, when the Irvines moved to Digby.

Mali Saeedi and Amir Tavassol had retired from the movie production business, sold their house in Niagara-on-the-Lake, Ontario, and were looking for somewhere in the Maritimes to settle. Amir was a producer/director and Mali was a cinematographer/editor. Their daughter, Dr. Panteha Tavassol, a recent medical graduate who loved big houses and big properties, had been doing research for them and indicated an interest in Cossaboom Corner.

In mid-February, through very hazardous driving conditions, Mali and Panteha drove to Nova Scotia to view the prospective property, were quarantined in Dartmouth for two weeks due to COVID-19, and, due to time constraints never reached Smith's Cove. They had been in contact with a Realtor and had seen pictures of Harbour View, and Panteha, who is interested in history, was aware of *The Harbour View Story* and the historic background of the property, which would make living at Harbour View a special privilege.

So, sight unseen from Ontario, they purchased the property. They are very happy they did and have found the local people very friendly.

Since their arrival Amir has been busy carrying out extensive renovations to the main floor areas, including both kitchens, the removal of some walls, extensive painting and papering and the addition of crown moulding throughout. Some of the rooms have been re-floored with porcelain tiles and the plan is to complete the entire apartment.

Outside, Amir has removed a number of trees to improve their view.

Near the pool

Near the pool

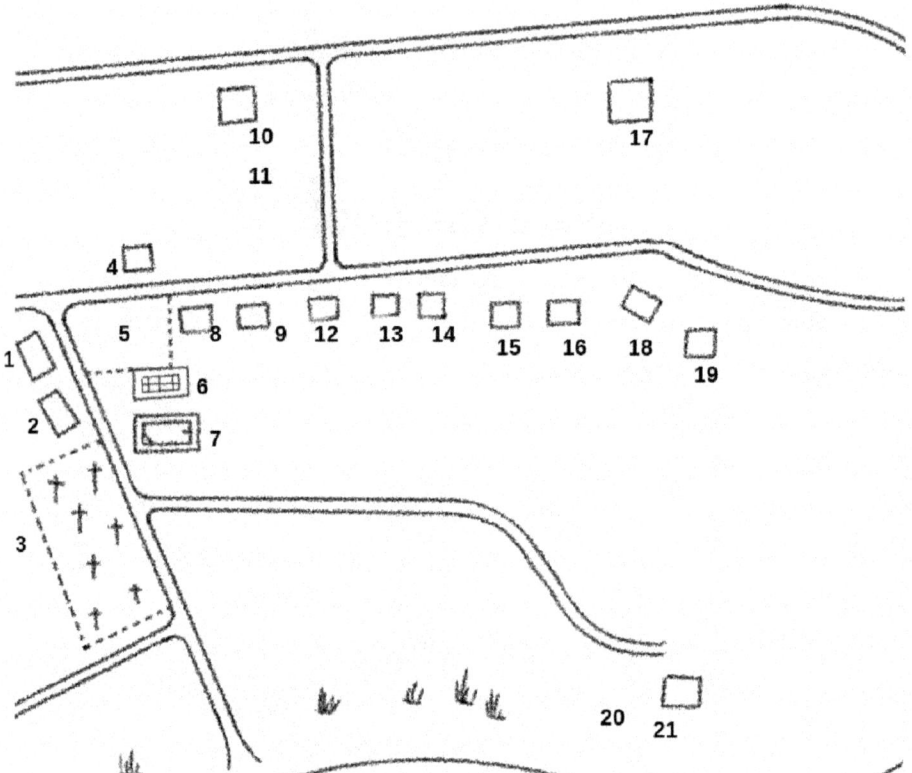

1	Emberlys'	12	Shady Grove
2	Langins'	13	Lessmore Cottage
3	Cemetery	14	Sunnymeade
4	Finally	15	North Point
5	Playground	16	New Dawn
6	Tennis	17	Tall Trees
7	Pool	18	Honey's Mouse House
8	Courtside Cottage	19	Cormore
9	Eagle's Nest	20	Quince Cottage
10	Linden Cottage	21	Mountains'
11	Summersrtock		

Emberlys'

6 Beachcomber Lane

The story of the Emberly family's ownership of the cottage next to the playground traces back to 1978, when Michael and Wendy, from Fall River, NS, accompanied by their sons Mark and Steven, joined the Harbour View community as owners after over a decade of annual family rental vacations at their summer haven.

Over the years, the landscape changed, property boundaries shifted, and friendships deepened, cul-

Best of Friends: Wendy Emberly and Jill Langin (circa 1990)

minating in the acquisition of the barn and the back duck pond with dear friends and neighbours Jill and Cliff Langin.

In the early 2000s, Mark and Elaine exchanged vows at the Birch Chapel, laying the groundwork for their own family's cherished memories at the cottage. With the arrival of their children, Marissa and Thomas, the Emberlys created their family stories of summer escapades and heartfelt moments of freedom and friendship with the next generation. Meanwhile, Steven and Debbie embarked on their own marital journey, and their children, Isabella and Gus, embraced the legacy of Harbour View, relishing the carefree joys and mischievous adventures of childhood.

Though Wendy passed away in 2014, her spirit remains alive in the Smith-Soulis Cemetery, where her grandchildren gather each Thanksgiving to collect chestnuts, a cherished tradition bridging generations.

As the Emberly clan thrived, the need for expansion arose, leading to a whimsical architectural project created by rum-induced inspiration and a simple sketch. An addition was added.

The grand architectural plan

The summers go by quickly, but they're packed with memories of laughter and cold drinks on the porch.

These "Harbour View Nights" nights are filled with cherished moments of friendship, late bedtimes for the kids and storytelling, almost overshadowing the late fish fry dinners that are served.

The Emberlys (Thanksgiving 2020) l-r: Isabella, Debbie, Steven, Gus, Thomas, Elaine, Marissa, Mark, Mike

Langins'

The Langins were first introduced to Harbour View in the summer of 1969, when the Smith family invited the Cliff, Jill, Glenn, and Holly to their cottage for a weekend. That weekend was spent enjoying all the activities that Harbour View had to offer, especially swimming and tennis.

They knew by the end of that weekend that they wanted a cottage in Harbour View. The timing could not have been better, as the Irvines Irvine had decided to sell several of the cottages. In 1970, the Langins, with the addition of baby Scott, purchased cottage #10, across from the pool and next to the graveyard.

For the past 54 years the Langins have considered cottage #10 to be a second home. Their family has grown to now include grandchildren and great-grandchildren who all live in Atlantic Canada and enjoy what Harbour View has to offer on a regular basis.

Rennee Woodworth (Holly's bestest friend), Jill Langin and Holly Langin having fun at the cottage

The Langins love entertaining and enjoying having friends spend the weekend with them at the cottage, so they thought a good way to remember those cherished weekends would be to invite friends and guests to write about their visit at Harbour View in a guest book. The first guest book started in 1970 and grew into a diary of the many memorable events that have been held at their cottage throughout the years. Additional books have been added over the years, with the tradition of writing in the guest book continuing to this day.

On those rainy days in Harbour View, the Langins enjoy reading through the diaries and reminiscing about those days gone by.

The Langin cottage was a "drop-in" centre in the early days, as kids would come for a pop from The Pop Shop that was in a vending machine in the kitchen, Allison Garber (MacLellan) and Jane

Hopgood were regulars.

Cliff and Jill have done many renovations to their cottage to accommodate their growing family and many friends who come to spend the weekend. In their early days at Harbour View, the roof of the Langin cottage was leaking and required a much-needed repair, which ended up with the whole roof being replaced. Jill decided on a red roof that Barry Cassidy of Bear River installed.

It was a change from the other cottages, being a very bright red metal roof. Langin neighbours Mike and Wendy Emberly started calling the cottage "Pizza Hut".

The largest renovation was undertaken in 2010 with a new kitchen and the addition of an eat-in area.

In January, 2000, Sylvia and David Irvine sold the land behind the Langin and Emberly cottages that ran from the graveyard up to the Harbour View Inn property. The Langins and Emberlys negotiated a price with David to purchase the land. The Langin portion included the barn and surrounding land up to the Emberly cottage, with the balance of the land going to the Emberlys.

At one time there was a duck pond on the land behind the cottages, but it was later filled in.

The Langins have been fortunate to have had several memorable occasions take place in Harbour View, with the first being the marriage of their daughter, Holly. Holly was married at St. Anne's Birch Chapel in Harbour View, followed by a reception held at the Mountain Gap Inn. A band was brought in from Halifax and played well past midnight for the enjoyment of relatives and guests alike.

Another memorable event held at Harbour View for the Langins was a surprise 50th wedding anniversary event (the surprise was for Jill) that took place over the course of a weekend in the fall of 2011, with about 50 family and friends attending. The invited guests were told that this was a surprise for Jill, and that all they had to do was get themselves to Harbour View, with Cliff taking care of all arrangements.

Cliff and Jill arrived Friday evening to a packed house at the Inn, much fun was had by all, with tears flowing from Jill and many others on the special occasion. Guests stayed at the Harbour View Inn

and other cottages in Harbour View, with a dinner and dance held at the Firemen's Hall in Smiths Cove. It was said that Cliff banked many "brownie points" that weekend.

To this day, Cliff Langin says that there were two great decisions that he made in his life. The first was marrying Jill Chalker, a true Newfoundlander; and the second was purchasing cottage #10 in Harbour View in 1970.

Finally

The evolution of the Carling family cottage, "Finally", over the years, as many of you know, is due in large part to our late mother, Joan, the unofficial matriarch of the Harbour View compound.

It has been and continues to be a little piece of heaven for the family, from the extensive gardens Joan lovingly tended, which her daughter Robin strives to maintain, to the wooden swing in the 'back Forty' where dear cottage friends still go to sit and chat with Mum—her spirit is prevalent everywhere on the property.

The cottage underwent an extensive renovation in 1997, with the kitchen being enlarged and a master bathroom installed; the original bathroom became a powder room. David Irvine's handiwork is evident in many of the finishing touches.

In 2004, the screened-in porch was added, essentially becoming an outdoor living room, and has hosted many get-togethers, from afternoon tea to post-pool time cocktails, and any number of luncheons and dinner parties.

The years following have seen the addition of various storage sheds on the property for the vast collection of gardening paraphernalia, as well as skylights in the main cottage.

"Finally" has always been a special place to relax and unwind in solitude from busy everyday life or a gathering place with family and friends for any and all occasions.

Courtside Cottage

70 Harbour View Road

The Wetmores brought a number of changes to Wetmore Place. The northwest wall used to end in a thicket of wild rose bushes. There is now a broad, open deck that connects to the covered porch, with a ramp to provide easy access.

The original kitchen was just large enough to make tea and toast for a family which was going to have most of its meals at the Inn, and was rendered even smaller by having a door toward the road that made the space more of a passageway than a kitchen. David Irvine remodelled one of the bedrooms into a kitchen of a size more appropriate for meal preparation and cleanup, and the former kitchen became a compact single bedroom.

During these renovations, a board bearing height markings for members of a family that used the then-smaller cottage (basically the rectangle ending where the porch roof ends, and without the two bedroom extensions on the side facing the road) during several summers between 1900 and 1910 was moved to a different lo-

The deck can hold a surprising number of people (2013)

cation and is no longer visible. However, the notations seem to be evidence that the cottage was in use at the start of operations of Harbour View House.

The main room had always seemed a little cave-like, but adding a skylight —and two more a decade later— brightened the space considerably. Following the example of the Langins, the Wetmores added a propane heater to the room that helped counter rough and chilly weather.

The single bathroom was often a point of anxiety when the cottage was full, especially if a number of children were present, and the addition of a powder room has improved cottage logistics significantly.

Bishop Stuart Wetmore baptized Nataleah Irvine in the Birch Chapel in 1990.

Frances Wetmore's artistic contributions included carving the chain of office that the President of the Harbourview Cottagers' Association wears on official occasions. Bishop Wetmore carved a large, shallow tray to hold an offering basket, and donated it to the Birch Chapel.

Five Wetmore family members share the ownership of what is now known as 'Courtside Cottage', and members of the extended family are most often in residence during August.

Three generations of Wetmores chasing soap bubbles

Eagle's Nest

76 Harbour View Road

The Kinsolving lot got a new cottage when part of cottage #18 was removed and relocated there. It was bought by Dr. Filbee of Halifax, and several years later he sold it to Edward and Charlotte McAniff of New York City, who renamed it "Eagle's Nest."

"Big Ed" McAniff was the retired former Chief of the New York City Fire Department, and Charlotte was a doctor of sharp mind but limited mobility, leading them to add some of the property's first accessibility features to the cottage.

The McAniffs were introduced to Harbour View by their daughter, Diane Clapp, who had moved to the nearby village of Bear River in 1978 with her husband, Harold, and two kids, Christian and Sam.

The Clapps themselves soon became part of the Harbour View community, renting various cottages on the property in the summer months and becoming enthusiastic participants in the weekly sailboat races in the Basin sponsored by the yacht club, while their kids grew up among a lively 1980s generation of Harbour View teenagers that included Langins, Emberlys, Corbetts, Webbs, Irvines, Carlings and Harpers.

When the McAniffs passed, the cottage was conveyed to the Clapp family. In 2005, after a decade living aboard a sailboat in the Caribbean, Diane and Harold returned to Harbour View and undertook a major renovation of the cottage.

The cottage nearly doubled in size and was fully winterized, as the Clapps became part of Harbour View's tiny but growing year-round population. Taking advantage of the property's sheltered location, the Clapps also planted a large garden in the field out front and added other features like trees and landscaping.

In 2013, the cottage was the site of one of the biggest parties ever seen at Harbour View, in honour of Harold's 70th birthday.

The Clapps' children, including daughter Christian and son-in-law Kasper Kovitz, remained frequent visitors to the property, and in 2015 their son Sam, daughter-in-law Thea Boyanowsky, and grandson Dmitri moved to nearby Annapolis Royal and became part of the Harbour View community themselves, renting the Klebert cottage at 208 Harbour View Road.

Linden Cottage

77 Harbour View Road

The Hopgood family (Chris, Mary Ellen, Jane, Geoff, Sarah and their beloved Dalmation, Perdy) purchased what was then known as "Linden Cottage" in 1980 and sold it to the Harwood family in 1996

The Hopgoods were at Harbour View from the last day of school each year until Labour Day weekend. Summers were a magical time punctuated by wonderful adventures. The Linden Cottage property had an overflowing flower garden and the flowers were put to good use in arrangements that were showcased at the Annual Digby Flower Show, under the tutelage of an incredible woman who lived in Smith's Cove, Mrs. Alice Oliver.

On the lower property the Hopgoods planted a vegetable garden which they managed to harvest from all summer long. The property also featured a pond which Chris Hopgood had dug out and named "Little Lake Mimi" in honour of Mary Ellen Hopgood's childhood summers spent on Lake Simcoe in Ontario.

The Hopgoods enjoyed all of the culinary delights of the local area. Mary Ellen would buy haddock from the pier at O'Neil's fishery in Digby that was so fresh it was practically still wiggling in the bag. Brown bread came from Christina's Bakery, a local staple that was located next to Ed's Fish and Chips on the way into Digby.

Vegetables and berries came from their own garden, and if extra berries were required for one of Mary Ellen's irresistible homemade pies, they were purchased from "The Strawberry Man", who sold top-notch produce out of his truck alongside the highway.

Long summer days held countless adventures from clam digging, to building forts, to door-to-door bake sales to earn money to buy treats at The Met and afternoons spent swimming in the pool and warming up lying on the tennis court.

The Harbour View Beach was also a favoured place to play. The family would take trips to Bear Island in an old wooden dory, purchased from Charles Turnbull, for picnics, and a few times a summer the Hopgood kids would team up with their friends to pick up garbage callously left behind on the beach, to earn a free slice of mud pie from Mona Webb at Harbourview Inn.

Jane, Geoff and Sarah knew it was time to come home when Mary Ellen rang a cow bell that could be heard throughout the property.

Once the sun was down, Mary Ellen would read classics to the Hopgood children by Linden Cottage's roaring fireplace, and then it was early to bed to rest up for another day of adventures.

Harbour View holds a special place in the hearts of all of the Hopgoods, and they all make time to visit each summer to reconnect with the memories and community they hold dear.

Summerstock

77 Harbour View Road

Victoria and Lee Harwood of Halifax acquired the cottage in 1996 and renamed it Summerstock. They had fallen in love with the tree-lined driveway that leads to a special family place.

Their daughters, Amanda, Lauren, Alexandra and Vienna, learned to swim, ride bicycles and appreciate nature in the Cove.

Over the years the Harwoods added their own touches, including a screened-in porch, an outdoor shower, a wood shed and a treehouse. Most of these projects were created by Kevin Hansen.

The mature trees and plantings, including a prolific wisteria, give the cottage a magical feeling. On beautiful and stormy days alike there is nothing more perfect than a day spent in the peace and quiet of Summerstock.

Shady Grove

82 Harbour View Road

Shady Grove in 1968

Shady Grove has been in Shawn Jolemore's family for nearly 30 years. Shawn's mother, Marilyn, and her then-husband, Gary, purchased the cottage in 1996 from the Bruce family, who were returning to live retirement life in their native Scotland.

While cottage #82 was new to them, Harbour View was not. Together with his parents (Ronnie and Marilyn), Shawn vacationed at cottage #10 in the summer of 1976 when he was just a toddler. The next summer they rented tiny cabin #16, which was known as the "Honeymoon" cottage (not to be confused with #6 Cottage

Lane, that also once had a small cottage called by that name).

The following year (1978), Shawn's parents jointly purchased cottage #122 from David Irvine. They spent many happy summers at that "Cormore" cottage, together with Corbett family relatives, right up until around 1995, when ownership transitioned to Shawn's cousin, Mark Corbett.

Interestingly, Shawn is also related to the Boyle family, who have owned #8 Chapel Lane since 1980.

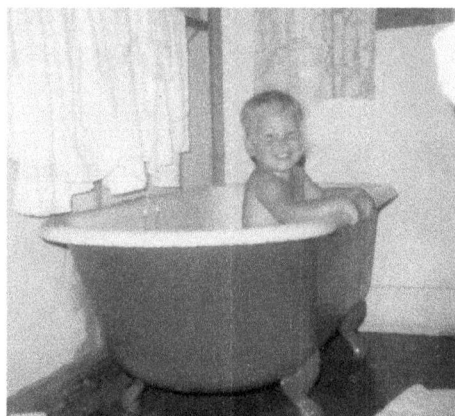

Shawn Jolemore in cottage #10 (Langins'), 1976.

Things were simpler in the 1980s and for a kid, summers seemed to last forever. The Harbour View compound provided the safety and freedom for children to roam, explore, and grow. Shawn learned to swim in the original (1947) concrete pool, ride his bike on the slate-covered roads (while evading "silent policeman"), become a proficient "port sail trimmer" on Uncle JJ's sailboat, and develop decent tennis skills on the old blacktop "short court".

Despite its unpredictable bounces and low chicken-wire fencing, that tennis court allowed for a wonderful introduction to the sport (and its accompanying "tennis tantrums"). And what's more, lying flat on the asphalt in the narrow doubles alley also helped the kids warm up after a swim.

For Shawn, Harbour View has also been the backdrop for the fleeting magic of adolescence. Formative memories include working the breakfast shift at "The Hotel" (under the watchful eye of Mona Webb), building forts with materials "borrowed" from Mr. Irvine, spying on the "big kids" at "the spot", raiding blueberry fields with Uncle Russ, and bartending (at only 15 years old) on the cottage happy hour circuit. Above all, though, coming of age at the cottage allowed for the forging of special friendships that have stood the test of time.

From 1996 to 2002, Shady Grove was a bustling spot filled with laughter and good cheer, where many of Marilyn and Gary's cherished friends would make annual summer visits.

Sadly, Gary died in 2004, before he could fulfill his creative vision for the place. But with generous help from David Irvine, and Gary's detailed blueprint, Shawn completed a "memorial balcony extension" the very next spring.

In the years that followed, ownership transitioned to Shawn. Extensive renovations took place around 2008, mainly to add a third bedroom to accommodate guests. Legend has it that in the Irvine years (or before) a section of the original building was removed and placed next door, to rent. Today, that piece comprises a central portion of Eagles' Nest, next door, and its owners find humour in the fact that Shawn completed a building renovation to add a room directly in the shadow of the original.

Shawn's partner, Tracey, first visited Harbour View around 2009. She recalls being immediately struck by the closeness of the community and how generations of families travel from all over the globe each summer to visit this little piece of paradise.

In 2012, Tracey and Shawn celebrated their nuptials at Harbour View, acknowledging its importance in their lives. They hosted a wedding weekend that featured fun and frolic at "The Barn", a ceremony at Saint Anne's "Birch" Chapel, and a reception at the Harbourview Inn. The couple incorporated a nod to Harbour View history at the reception, serving a signature drink called the "Imbertville Station", in reference to the name of a 1924 railway station stop "only 50 feet from Harbour View limits".

Tracey and Shawn's son made his inaugural visit to Shady Grove around 2016 and, in the years that have followed, is experiencing the same special qualities that Harbour View cottage life offered his dad. Tracey and Max now take up residence each summer for much of July and August.

As for Shawn, he can often be found sitting beneath the shade of the veranda's extended hipped roof, tucked up underneath a kitchen window, looking out at the sea. It's the same window from where, in 1969, a young Douglas Irvine and his teenage friends served up "Shady Dogs" and "Grove Burgers" to swimmers who'd stroll over from the pool to grab a bite at the "Shady Grove Canteen".

Shawn loves sharing nostalgic stories like that. They help him convey his deep connection to a place that has largely remained the same even as its inhabitants come and go. He also loves the idea that his son may someday continue to uphold the laid-back ambience of "The Grove" and the family tradition of summer life at Harbour View.

Shady Grove in 2012

Lessmore Cottage

88 Harbour View Road

Cottage 88 in the 1970s

Cottage #88 never really had a name that stuck. For a time in the 1980s, the MacLean family hung a tole-painted sign outside the roadside door that read *Tigh Na Mara*, which is Gaelic for "View of the Sea".

In 1991, following consecutive summer rental stays, Jane Lessel purchased the humble, two-bedroom cabin from the MacLeans and enjoyed its splendid sea views for nearly 30 years.

As with many inhabitants of Harbour View, Jane's family ties to the cottage community go back a long way. Her grandmother, Mrs. Graves, once owned cottage #17, and Jane has a photograph of her two-year-old self, with an inscription that reads "Janie in a field at Harbour View".

An accomplished rug hooker, Jane was a member of the "Smith's Cove Happy Hookers" and has gifted or sold many of her pieces throughout the region. She began to learn the art and craft of rug hooking after her retirement, during what she calls her "most favourite September".

Later, Jane's partner, Dave Faloon, joined her at Harbour View. They were married in Digby in 2001, and their attendants were Phil and Mona Webb (then owners of the Harbourview Inn) with officiant (and Dave's local sailing friend) Judge Charles Haliburton.

Jane and Dave would take up residence in early Spring and stay through to Thanksgiving, which was marked by an annual cottagers' dinner at the Inn. While Jane enjoyed the advantages of the "old" swimming pool (she never liked the "new" one quite as much), Dave could be found tinkering and puttering around the cottage yard. An avid gardener, he held an annual "growing contest" with neighbour Charles Turnbull for who could grow the tallest sunflowers, and once tried (with limited success) growing grapes on a small trellis fence in the lower field.

Dave and Jane also enjoyed entertaining regular summer guests, including hosting annual visits from Dave's family, who would travel by ferry from Saint John.

They never got around to officially naming the cottage but did consider the uniquely-spelled "Shaddows", a name found imprinted on an antique cottage sundial passed down from Jane's grandmother. That would have been a fitting name given the shadows cast by the massive maple trees that once encircled the place.

The cottage is now owned by the Jolemore family. Extensive renovations were completed to the building around 2021, along with considerable landscaping to better transition with their neighbouring property to the south. In the spirit of Harbour View, the building remains unassuming and retains much of the rustic charm and history of the place.

The Jolemores use the cottage for guests, including Shawn's mother, Marilyn, who now takes up residence there in summer. Marilyn has a long history at Harbour View, and values returning to her "healing place" to bond with her grandson and watch him explore, learn, and grow just as she did with her own son more than a generation ago.

A new nameplate, *Lessmore Cottage,* acknowledges the transition of ownership from one family to the next, coupled with a nod to how the current owners feel about the enduring quality of the larger cottage community.

Harbour View is a place where small traditions and ways of being can mean a lot, where you can choose to unplug from the distractions of a digitally-driven lifestyle and connect to its unique quality of summer life. It's a place where less *is* more.

Lessmore Cottage, 2021

Sunnymeade

94 Harbour View Road

Detail from a painting by Charles Turnbull.

The cottage name dates back to its construction in 1928. For nearly a century now, the place has maintained its original vibe and its original purpose: as a place for friends and family to gather, enjoy the camaraderie of one another and the local community, and take in the views and low-key lifestyle that hearkens back to earlier days, when times seemed freer and life was in many ways more simple. If that is the purpose of a seasonal summer cottage, then Sunnymeade has served valiantly and never wavered.

As one of the cottages owned solely by descendants of its original owners, Sunnymeade has served as a family gathering spot consistently over the years. While not always particularly easy or quick to get to by most of the family, a visit there has always been worth the trip. With family visiting from locations as disparate as Boston, West Virginia and San Francisco in the US, and Rothesay and Vancouver in Canada, the reward of time at the cottage has consistently exceeded any travel headaches. In fact, it has faithfully proven to provide a quick cure for them.

It was originally constructed by Caroline T. Hanson (born in Gardiner, Maine and who spent her adult life in East Orange, New Jersey). Ownership was transferred upon her passing in 1953 to her only child, Marjorie Hanson Turnbull (Mrs. William Wallace Turnbull) of South Orange, NJ. Ownership was subsequently transferred upon her passing in 1974 to the oldest of her three sons, Charles Hanson Turnbull. It then became jointly owned by Charles and his wife, Priscilla, from Old Lyme and Niantic, Connecticut, and then subsequently by their three children: Linda, David and Wendy. Over the years, ownership passed solely to David of the North Shore of Massachusetts.

The cottage retains virtually all of its original character, with the exception of the kitchen, which by design had been tiny because, until sometime in the 1970s, the family took all their meals at the Harbour View House. During its first half century the kitchen never had to serve as a place other than to house an icebox and a sink, or for many other purposes than to prepare cocktails. Without changing its size, Dave Irvine did the work of updating it in 1974, which was his first kitchen renovation.

The kitchen remains the same today. It is still tiny, but very functional, though it still lacks a mechanical dishwasher, meaning that all of the dishes are washed and dried by hand. This task is usually undertaken by two people—not because it wouldn't be great to have others help to lighten the load, but rather because that's pretty much the capacity of the room. At other times, when a helper cannot be engaged (or be trusted not to drop the wine glasses), it can be a lonely, albeit contemplative, task.

Despite its lack of size, the kitchen has produced some of the most memorable meals ever—mostly eaten out-of-doors on the covered veranda by parents, children, grandchildren, spouses and friends of every denomination. While after fifty years the kitchen could use some updating, the output from it could not be improved!

The view of the cove, the meadow, the Basin, the mouth of Bear River, the hillside and beyond serves as an always-changing backdrop to life on the veranda. And its proximity to the pool and tennis court ensures there is never an excuse—or, at least, not a *good* excuse—not to get a bit of exercise and a visit with other cottagers (which, in and of itself, occasionally prevents one from getting any exercise).

In keeping with the themes of tradition and simplicity, the cottage has white cedar shakes, the same as do so many other traditional structures found in coastal Nova Scotia. The beauty of the shakes is that they change over time under the influence of sun, rain and salt air to a silvery gray, a colour that is tough to match, and with an overall aesthetic that's tough to beat. White cedar offers beauty and simplicity and requires virtually no maintenance. The original shingles on the south and west sides of Sunnymeade didn't have to be replaced for a little over 90 years.

The cottage has had a stream of family visiting every summer, with the notable exceptions of World War II and the first summer of the COVID pandemic. It has consistently served as a restorative, centring place to connect, and re-connect, yet again.

It has also served as a place for celebrating and for commemorating. Birthdays, anniversaries, graduations, honeymoons, a wedding, job changes and events of many other varieties have been celebrated at the cottage over the years, building one on another a trove of memories and serving to chronicle the milestones of those who frequent it most. And, too, it has also served as a place for commemoration, such as the family gathering to celebrate the life of the cottage's longest resident, Charles Hanson Turnbull who passed away in 2016 and whose spirit still lives within its walls.

Summer cottages are a special treat. And, too, summer communities are a special treat, and the one shared by all the cottagers at Harbour View is something to cherish and preserve.

The traditions of both cottage and community are of incalculable value and have served to provide all of its members with a blessing that would be difficult to duplicate elsewhere.

North Point

102 Harbour View Road

David Turnbull's lifelong affection and loyalty to Harbour View have been matched by his wife, Suzie, ever since they spent their honeymoon at the Sunnymeade Cottage in 1980. That honeymoon started a nearly unbroken series of happy summer visits to Sunnymeade to stay with Charles and Priscilla for the next seventeen years, with every bed in the cottage filled with three generations of Turnbulls.

When Carol and Stan Nelson decided in 1996 to sell the cottage that was right next door to Sunnymeade, it seemed like the perfect opportunity to spread out the extended Turnbull family while retaining the fun of being together. David and Suzie say it was one of the best decisions they ever made because their original vision has played out exactly as they hoped ever since, with constant traffic wearing out the grass path between the two cottages.

Naming the cottage was one of the first things David and Suzie did. Everyone loved the Sunnymeade name and it only seemed right that this new cottage have a distinctive name, too. They settled on 'North Point', first because it was their family's special northern home, and second because it was the same name as the beautiful small publishing company founded by David's uncle and Charles' brother, Bill Turnbull.

Charles and Priscilla were excited about the prospects for the cottage, too, and even before David and Suzie came up in the summer of 1997, they ambitiously tackled the job of clearing the dense spruces and shrubs that had created a veritable wall between the cottages.

In need of immediate attention was the porch, which had fallen into disrepair. Previous owners had modified it so that only half was under roof and David and Suzie wanted to restore it to its original form.

In addition to reroofing the open deck area, they moved the steps from the centre of the porch to the south end, which old pictures proved was their original position. This meant there was a direct line of only about 40 feet to Sunnymeade's porch steps, guaranteeing busy movement between the two cottages from the beginning.

The last part of the porch restoration was a new peeled-pole railing enclosing the whole space, making for the fantastic outdoor room where most of the family's summer living takes place.

The interior remains almost exactly the same as when the Turnbulls bought it, with the exception that the kitchen was updated with new cabinets and counters. The bedrooms and bathrooms are so close to how they originally were that when the granddaughter of the man who built the cottage rented it one summer, she remarked that her view up to the rafters when lying in the bathtub was the same one she remembered as a girl.

A portrait of the deck by Rebekah Wetmore. The painting opens in the middle to reveal the view of the Basin from the deck.

Some years after they purchased North Point, Suzie and David noticed apparent outward movement of the exterior walls, and, copying what had previously been done at Sunnymeade, they installed cables across the interior of the cottage to connect the front and back walls. The cables were encased in wood to mimic rafters.

A major change was replacing the original half logs on the exterior with white cedar shingles. It was remarkable that the exterior had remained unchanged since the cottage was built in 1910, but gaps in the logs were allowing liberal amounts of cold air and mosquitoes into the place and the bottom of many of the logs had become water-damaged and rotten.

Shortly after the cottage was purchased, the window frames were painted green to match Sunnymeade's, but after the shingling job, Suzie and David chose to repaint the frames more of a moss green.

Over the years the roof has been replaced twice and the top of the chimney rebuilt with sturdier brick. Over the summer of 2023 the inside of the fireplace was repaired and the chimney finally got a cap on it.

The best part of the story of the chimney repair is that the mason, Lester Saulnier, had to shimmy down the inside of the chimney from the roof to get into the cottage because it hadn't been unlocked for him. Santa Claus comes to Harbour View!

The *rosa rugosa* hedge along the road was laboriously created one summer by Suzie and her kids by planting slips of the pink variety dug up from the Sunnymeade hedge, and of the white variety from Jane and Dave Faloon's shrubs. It has done so well that it has almost completely eclipsed the huge mint bed that was there before and was the base for son Doug's famous mint juleps.

At the time David and Suzie bought the cottage, their children, Elizabeth, Douglas and Caroline, were 14, 12 and 8, respectively. Until the COVID summers of 2020 and 2021, there wasn't a summer that they didn't each manage to make the trip to "everyone's favourite place on earth," to quote from a collage of photos that Elizabeth once made.

A measure of how much the Turnbull children love the place is how often they have invited friends to enjoy the cottage. Each of them brought their prospective spouses up, too, to make sure they would pass the "cottage test"!

They certainly all did, and, in Caroline's case, her husband Kyle agreed it would be a great place for their honeymoon. At this writing, each of the three Turnbull children have three children of their own, and Suzie and David's grandchildren—Iris, Charlie and Douglas Henry; Suzanna, Molly and Emma Turnbull; and Franny, Wallace and Eliza Doran—are now weaving their own experiences into the old and familiar patterns.

What's best about being there? To quote family members themselves, "The porch, outside in the fresh air all day; sense of calm looking out over the cove and the meadow; being in sync with the weather, the breezes and the tides; family meals *al fresco*, with simple, fresh food; cousin time; daybed sitting for reading, games, conversation and cocktails; sleeping; frying fish and making bread; hearing cannonballs from the pool and the delayed thump of tennis balls from the court; friends and community."

What David and Suzie love best about the cottage is that, in a world that is constantly changing, there is a simple spot on a beautiful meadow that has changed very little, and that their children and grandchildren treasure it as much as they do.

New Dawn

104 Harbour View Road

Beginning with Hugh and Judy Smith's honeymoon at Harbour View in 1967, (the year the Irvines bought the resort), they had a deep appreciation for the entire "Harbour View experience".

They purchased Cottage #25 in the fall of 2000 and, although the family had a longstanding connection to the area, this cottage was new to them.

Hugh and Judy initially owned the cottage now referred to as North Point and enjoyed summers there with their children, Whipple, Amy, Jamie, Victoria, and Katie. They all still frequently visit with their families.

The Smiths' memories include sailing to Goat Island, Hugh's Sunday mornings with Kelsey Raymond to talk about the sailing course that he raced every week in his P20, the children's program run by Nancy and Bizzy included fun games and music played by Bizzy in the barn, beach bonfires and frog hunting behind the chapel.

A highlight for Whipple and Amy was being on a float in the Bear River Cherry Festival, and making flower arrangements with Mrs. Oliver and entering them in the Digby Pines Flower show.

Jamie, Shawn and Stephen were always up to adventures that started aboard Lloyd's tractor and ended up with many makeshift fort constructions and stolen matches.

Katie and Victoria remember beach-combing, suntanning and walks to the Inn for treats and the newspaper. Who can forget the classic Louisville Slugger squirrel take down at breakfast by Hugh Smith?

The cottage served as a summer gathering spot for the Smith family, and in 2003, they expanded it to include a bunk house with three bedrooms and a bathroom. A new master bedroom and en-suite was also added to accommodate more family members.

The interior of the cottage features beautiful paintings by Grandma Judy; some are her version of Maud Lewis' classics—lovingly referred to by the family as "Fraud Lewis".

Over the years, the family created cherished memories of campfires, s'mores, dance parties and field games with all of the cousins, rainy day visits to Frenchy's and all the drama around the bats flying around the cottage at night are classic cottage memories. The MacAskill children loved visiting their great grandmother Nana on her back deck with a special McLobster take out meal, and dressing up to attend the strawberry shortcake tea celebration held annually at the Smiths Cove Museum.

Wallace and Amy took over ownership of the cottage in 2020 and renamed it "New Dawn", as a tribute to the roses Hugh and Judy planted and symbolic of new beginnings. Their four children—Meghan, Hugh, Sarah, and James—enjoyed their cottage summers with family and friends spending time together and enjoying activities like relaxing at the pool, searching for sea glass, attempting to

l-r: Sarah, Meghan, James and Hugh MacAskill enjoying the pool area in 2007.

dig for clams, biking, playing tennis, naps on the "Nelsons'" deck chaise longue and exploring with their friends.

Special memories are the Frenchies formal, summer jobs at the Harbourview Inn, biking to McDonalds and Jaggars Point to get treats before playing mantracker and camouflage, building a fort on the beach (and getting stuck at high tide) games of colours in the pool, the annual pool party, babysitting and lemonade stands. The highlight was a trip to the Kings Theatre in Annapolis Royal for the one and only movie of the summer and a trip to Upper Clements Park after earning a Fast Pass by participating in the Digby Library summer reading program.

Recently, the MacAskill family has extended their cottage season, with their children now all young adults. Wallace and Amy enjoy morning coffee, beach walks for sea glass, bike rides, pickleball, paddleboarding, golfing, gardening, dips in the basin and pool time with the next generation of Harbour View families. Trips to Lazy Bear, Annapolis Royal, and Bear River for coffee are their favourite weekly destinations. They can't wait to arrive in April and are sad to leave in October.

The MacAskill family look forward to continuing the tradition of the cottage as a place of family connection and the Harbour View experience, now in the fourth generation.

Quince Cottage and the boathouse

Beachcomber Lane

Included with the Harbour View property, purchased by the Irvines in 1967 was a small cottage that, in 1980 was separated into two pieces, transported to and along the beach to the site of a former Sulis homestead, and reconnected to become a summer home for the next 15 years for the Irvines. The former cottage #4 became 21 Beachcomber Lane.

In 1989 the Irvines sold the property across from the Inn to the Webbs and moved to Beachcomber Lane as their year-round home. Situated on the brow of a gentle slope toward the Annapolis Basin, Quince Cottage, after a number of renovations, showed no sign of its unpretentious beginnings.

Nestling into that slope, from the circular paved driveway to the west it deceivingly appeared to be a bungalow fronted by a large brick patio, with a wooden deck snaking around the corner to the south. But from the water side it appeared as an expansive, two level, multi-decked building, with many large windows and doors.

The continuous deck linked the main entrance to four areas that could accommodate groups of various sizes. These included a sheltered, sunny spot off the kitchen, the screened porch off the master bedroom, and the aptly-named "Flying Bridge" for larger gatherings.

The fourth area, reached by a set of stairs, was the sizable gazebo, built in 1994 by various members of the Irvine family to be the site of Jenny's wedding. A few years later, the gazebo was skidded over and attached to the deck.

Named after the impressive quince bush that adorned the waterside lawn, planted by the original homesteading Sulis family who settled on the land in the late 1700s, the building was situated so that every room, except the two bathrooms, faced east. This provided expansive views through large picture windows of the Basin down to Goat Island and the gentle sweep of the shore around Sulis Cove.

One entered through the substantial wooden door, adorned with an operable port hole, and immediately had a view of the Basin, past the picture-galleried stairs to the lower level and through one of two immense picture windows in the living room.

The single window in the bedroom facing north allowed one to lie in bed and savour a splendid view across a wide expanse of lawn, over two ponds and finally across the Basin to the extreme tip of Bear Island.

Like Topsy, the building grew with numerous renovations over the years, from its humble beginning, into an extremely user-friendly home, with kitchen, master bedroom and dining room all opening into the living room and entry hall from various directions. The small but serviceable kitchen was centred by an island that was once an oak, glass-fronted display case in downtown Digby's Levy's Drug Store.

The lower level duplicated the upper, without a kitchen but with a hot tub, large shower and mini-gym, all well windowed to the east.

Before the Irvines sold the Inn to the Webbs, the former laundry building that was Mrs. Stella Rhyno's domain, at the back of the Inn, was declared superfluous. Like so many other buildings previously, it was jacked up, put on skids and hauled down the road to the shore, to be the boathouse at Quince Cottage.

Each fall, before the sloop "Argonaut" was winched in for the winter, the double doors were opened and the sailing families of the Royal Western Nova Scotia Yacht Club held their end-of-season party on the beach. Prizes for the summer races were awarded, along with very special sailing related drawings by local artist, sailor and self proclaimed "Admiral", Kelsey Raymond. The Irvines are fortunate to have a number of these drawings that are cherished, reminding them of their close friendship with that very special man.

A beach party at the boat house

After the Irvine sailboats no longer fit in the boathouse, the big double doors were replaced by a window, and first Geoff and then Jenny Irvine and Karla Corbett used it as a bunky during summer employment while at University.

Over the years a number of major alterations were made to the property surrounding Quince Cottage, including the construction of three ponds, the paving of the driveway, the development by Sylvia of a large number of attractively harmonious gardens and the placing of rock rip-rap in an effort to lessen the rapid erosion of the shore front.

The boathouse and Quince Cottage

In 2010 the Irvines sold Quince Cottage to the Mountains, who tore it down and replaced it with a house of their choice. This spelled the end of Harbour View Cottage #4 at 21 Beachcomber Lane.

Although the wood shed was included in the sale of Quince to the Mountains, they graciously offered it to the Irvines and it was skidded next door to their unnumbered lot. The rustic sign by the road refers to it as "The Woodshed", and in it the Irvines store life jackets, oars, the outboard motor, a kayak and summer beach fire-pit paraphernalia.

Another item salvaged from Quince Cottage was the very substantial front door, mentioned earlier. Lovingly fashioned by their good friend Tony Voegele, an Austrian master carpenter, the door now graces Julie and Geoff Irvine's home in Jollimore, a unique area of Halifax.

Mountains'

21 Beachcomber Lane

Jim and Joanne Mountain were introduced to Harbourview in 1998 by the Harwoods, who had recently bought their cottage on the property. Over the next twelve years the Mountains and their then-young children, William and Adrienne, were frequent guests of the Harwoods at Harbourview, and the family developed a great appreciation for the community and the setting.

In 2010, on a visit to the Cove, Jim and Joanne learned that 21 Beachcomber Lane, Dave and Sylvia Irvine's house, was for sale. Without a great deal of forethought, they agreed to purchase the property. And while much thought went into a possible renovation, they decided to build the new house that stands there today. In 2012, Jim and Joanne spent their first summer in the new house.

When it came time to landscape around the new house, Lee Harwood introduced them to Kevin Hansen, who was their part-time gardener and handyman. Kevin, a rugged individualist who lived completely off the grid, didn't work for just anybody, but the Mountains passed 'the interview' and work began.

Kevin Hanson

The dry stack rock retaining wall that stands as of this writing was Kevin's doing, and from there he went on to become the *de facto* caretaker of the property. In the ensuing years, Kevin worked on special projects for other Harbour View families. He built a camp on the Mountains' property in 2016, where he lived until his death in March of 2021.

21 Beachcomber Lane holds many fond memories of friendship, fellowship, community, and family.

Tall Trees

92 Jaggar Lane

Built 1919 for Dr. and Mrs. Daniel (Alma) Turner of New York on land purchased from Bishop Jaggar, and therefore technically not originally a part of Harbour View.

Daniel Lawrence Turner was chief engineer of New York City's Transit Construction Commission, and oversaw a comprehensive rapid transit plan covering all boroughs of the city.

A graduate of Norfolk (Virginia) Academy and Rensselaer Polytechnic Institute, Dr. Turner travelled globally lecturing on city engineering and urban planning. He was appointed by President Hoover to represent the United States at the 1929 World Engineering Congress in Japan.

Tall Trees was designed by Turner and built by Ralph Cossitt us-ing Douglas fir, transported from British Columbia, throughout the interior. Dr. Turner chaired the committee that designed St. Anne's Birch Chapel, also built by Mr. Cossitt, and the extensive use of white birch in the chapel is also a distinctive feature on all the mouldings, cabinet trim and stairway fixtures in Tall Trees.

An exterior deck originally ran the length of the northwestern side of the cottage, adjacent to a lawn bowling green, a favourite pastime for the Turners and their guests. That deck was later replaced by a two story exterior deck, wrapped in wisteria. The Turners were avid landscape gardeners and a number of ornamental trees still remain on the property. The bowling green is now simply referred to as the "side lawn".

After World War II, Tall Trees was sold by the Turner estate to Mr. and Mrs. Walter W. (Dorothy) Flett for use as their summer home while they owned the hotel.

The Fletts enclosed the covered deck on the northeast side of the cottage overlooking the meadow, which was the main pathway approach at the time, with windows and screens to create an all-weather prospect to view the cove.

After the sale of the hotel, the Fletts sold Tall Trees to Dr. Jack and Audrey Charman of Halifax. It was owned by Mrs. Charman until her passing in 1998.

Audrey Charman was a popular and active resident of Harbour View who enjoyed gardening, golf and especially entertaining. Considered the matriarch of Tall Trees, she was regularly joined by her children, David (Doreen) and Judy (Peter) MacLellan, and her seven grandchildren, throughout the summer and autumn seasons.

Upon her passing, Tall Trees was bequeathed to Audrey Charman's daughter, Judy, who, with husband Peter, continued to enjoy Smiths Cove and would become permanent summer residents.

Over the next two decades Judy assumed the matriarchal role, adding extensive gardens and making interior upgrades to the original facilities. Searching far and wide, she would eventually locate reclaimed Douglas fir cabinetry and make major renovations to the kitchen and other aspects of the interior woodwork.

The MacLellans in 2017

Throughout the seasons Judy and Peter were regularly joined by their three children, all of whom loved their summers at Harbour View and made lifelong friends. Each eventually would enjoy wedding celebrations there, and now their children add new voices to the summer activities.

Son Scott and his wife Ryoko (Mitsuyasu) live in in Forest Hills, NY, with a home in Stowe, VT as well. They have two sons, Lauchlan and Spencer.

Son Jamie and his wife Claudia (Chender) live in Dartmouth (HRM) NS with their three children: twin daughters Molly and Ana, and son Sam.

Daughter Allison and husband Jeff (Garber) reside in Bedford (HRM) NS and have two children, son Hugh and daughter Vera.

Throughout a protracted illness Judy, assisted by Peter, continued to add to the landscaping and interior beauty of Tall Trees, while delighting in the company of their children and grandchildren. Judy passed away in 2019 and was placed to eternal rest in Smith-Sulis cemetery at Harbour View, next to her mother, Audrey.

Ownership of the cottage passed to Peter and the children, who continue to enjoy the seasons and fellowship offered by their special place.

The main room, with the enormous fireplace

Honey's Mouse House

114 Harbour View Road

Honey Shields became friends with Lynn Odell when they both worked on a health fair at New York University Medical Center, and they took to having lunch once a week. They had just finished the event in 1990 and Honey had had a very stressful month: her father had died very suddenly and her nephew had been born with medical complications.

Lynn took one look at Honey at lunch and told her that she (Honey) looked like garbage and had a choice: she could either go

91

to Nova Scotia voluntarily or Lynn would kidnap her.

Honey went to Nova Scotia.

When they got to Lynn's cottage, Honey went out to the porch and saw the panoramic view of Smith's Cove—from Digby Gut and all the way up toward Annapolis Royal. She took a deep breath and burst into tears. Nova Scotia became her healing place!

It was during that first trip that David Irvine took Lynn and Honey sailing around Bear Island, where they saw seals, loons, harbour porpoises and egrets. Being from the Bronx, Honey was used to seeing such creatures only at the zoo, if at all. It made her determined to get a place in Smiths Cove.

That same year, there was a cottage that had just sold up the hill from Lynn's. Honey had missed her chance by just a few weeks.

Then, in 1991, another cottage became available: 114 Harbour View. It was decorated in lots of orange, a colour neither Lynn nor Honey was fond of, but they saw past it and Honey made an offer. it. A deal was struck and she has never regretted it since.

Honey had brought up a couch that opened into a queen size bed. When a friend came to visit, they went to open the bed, only to find a nest of mice in the mattress.

Honey ran out of the cottage with her arms waving over her head, screaming to get the mice out. Her friend got them out and they moved the mattress out to the lawn.

Lynn told Honey that she would have to desensitize herself to her fear of mice. "Think of Mickey Mouse," she said.

Everyone started giving Honey decorations, art, bedding and linens featuring mice. Her cottage was soon called dubbed "The Mouse House," with a Mickey Mouse sign made by Marshall Webb. She also had a little cement sailor named after the friend who gave it to her, "Sam".

The first renovation was to the back porch. The boards were so warped that Lynn was afraid to step out on it. The cottage is built on a steep hill so the front is at ground level, but the back is held up by beams. The existing ones had nearly rotted away and had to be replaced.

The home improvements lasted many years. Redoing the roof.

Taking out alders to clear the view. Building a shed for tools and gardening supplies. Planting lilacs to replace the trees near the road. Renovating and insulating the master bedroom. Moving the door between the master bedroom and the porch and installing a sliding door that gives a perfect view of the sun rising. Installing and camouflaging a washer and dryer in the second bedroom. Adding ceiling fans, replacing the electrical wiring and putting air conditioning in the two bedrooms.

One of the thornier issues was the chimney, which kept leaking. It was on the diagonal in the living room, making it impossible to get to the back. When the cottage walls were opened up to put a beam under the kitchen, it was discovered that there was sand at the bottom of the chimney (in the old days, apparently, they used sand from the beach to mix cement). After 80 years, the cement no longer held up. So, the new project entailed replacing the chimney and re-shingling the cottage.

Lynn's first trip up was when she was three, in 1947. One of her earliest memories was of wanting to go sailing. Admiral Shenstone promised he would take her when she got her certificate for swimming and when she got it, she couldn't even talk, she was so excited. She just held up the certificate and he took her aboard.

For 29 years Lynn and Honey would come up twice a year "off-season". Many of those years Ellen McClelland, Dee Nelson and other friends would join the visit.

Often the first night (and many other nights) involved a welcoming dinner at Marylou and Kelsey Raymond's. After dinner, Marylou and Lynn would work on a crossword puzzle or Marylou would tell stories about families in the cove. She was the Ancestry.com of Smith's Cove.

Lynn and Honey worked with Marylou on projects for the Smith's Cove Historical Society. One project, inspired by a fundraiser Honey had organized in New York City, resembled a walkathon but involved sailboats. There was a prize for the winner of the race as well as for the person who raised the most money. Nova Scotia Yacht Club ran the sail and volunteers from the museums ran the silent auction, regular auction, dinner and tea.

It became a yearly weekend event for almost 25 years, raising thousands of dollars for the Digby Museum and the Smith's Cove Museum.

Ellen McClelland made another important find. Marylou had told us that Honey's cottage had been rented for years by Ms. Bell and Ms. Runyon. It turned out that Dorothy M. Bell was president of Bradford Junior College from 1940 until her retirement in 1967. She was the College President when Ellen was there. Jane Runyon was the College Secretary and Registrar. The two of them shared the President's House at the college. She retired at the same time as Miss Bell.

Miss Runyon (standing) and Miss Bell

At the time, it never occurred to the students that Miss Bell and Miss Runyon might be a couple. In the '60s it wasn't considered quite proper for an unmarried woman to live alone.

Upon her (their) retirement, Miss Bell said the first thing she/they were going to do was spend a good long time in Nova Scotia.

Ellen never gave it another thought until David Irvine asked if Ellen had heard anyone call a cast iron frying pan a "spider." (She had.) He went on to say that was the term "the girls", Miss Bell and Miss Runyon, used. They would take a "spider" with them to cook lunch over a fire on an outing to Bear Island. Not only were they regulars at Harbour View, but they always rented Honey's cottage!

Cormore

122 Harbour View Road

For the Corbett family, a simple stroll along the roads of Harbour View can bring back 50 years of memories. It might be the familiar smell of the flowers, or the feel of the road beneath their feet, a certain tree, or the sight of a long-forgotten rock wall. Whatever it is, they know the feeling: it's familiar, timeless, and welcoming.

Their deep connection to Harbour View began in the mid-1970s when John, Marilyn, and their young children, Mark and Karla, rented cottages #10 and #18 (now #82) for successive summers, before acquiring #30 (now #122) in 1978. At the time, they'd considered other cabins that fit their family of four, but David Irvine suggested that they think about co-purchasing the larger #30 together with their Jolemore family relatives (Ronnie, Marilyn, and Shawn), who were also looking to buy. The two closely-knit families jumped at the chance and that was the start of many happy

95

summers together at *Cormore*.

Harbour View provided the backdrop for countless summer adventures and activities for Mark, Karla, and Shawn. The cousins recall participating in the Children's Program at the Barn (run by Nancy and Bizzy Prescesky), riding on Geoff and Jenny Irvine's ponies, purchasing popsicles and "penny candies" at Aunt Minerva's Store, and savouring a slice of Mona's "mud pie" at "the Big House". There were also fun annual events to look forward to, like Smith's Cove "Good Times Day" (with its dunk tank), the Bear River Cherry Carnival (with its parade and unique greasy-pole competition), and the Harbour View cottagers' pool party. Later memories include parties on Bear Island, and working restaurant shifts at the Inn.

Through it all, though, the old swimming pool and tennis court remained the fixtures of summer life at the cottage. It seemed like everyone learned to swim and play tennis there and Mark recalls being part of many competitive tennis matches on that court, much to the delight of the Wetmore cottage inhabitants, who had permanent courtside seats. Karla also remembers quiet nights when you'd suddenly hear the loud roar of the Irvines' truck speeding toward the pool, followed by bright flashlights and the scattering of teens who had snuck in to swim after dark.

Sailing was also an important part of summer life for the Corbetts. John grew up boating on Nova Scotia's Prospect Bay, but later, as an adult, discovered the Annapolis Basin (with its changing tides) to be the better training ground for sailing. He regularly crewed aboard David Irvine's *Argonaut* and Kelsey Raymond's *Come by Chance* for Sunday and Wednesday races.

Then, starting in 1985, John skippered his own Westwind Paceship boat, *Kar-la-mel*, in weekly races on the Basin. Crew was never in short supply with Mark, Karla, Shawn, and friends available at a moment's notice. Also, John's boat could be moored right off the Harbour View beach because it was equipped with a retractable centreboard, so could safely sit flat in the mud at low tide.

John still occasionally sails the Basin, but now it's aboard his son Mark's boat.

The late 1990s and early 2000s welcomed the next cottage generation in the form of Karla's daughter, Mayev, and Mark and Carrie's children, Leah and Conner. Much like their parents before them, they have grown up with the amazing experiences and special memories that summer life offers, including cottage morning routines with "Grampy JJ", biking adventures, beach parties, summer birthday celebrations, and lifelong friendships forged on the Harbour View playground.

At the pump house

At the Pump house

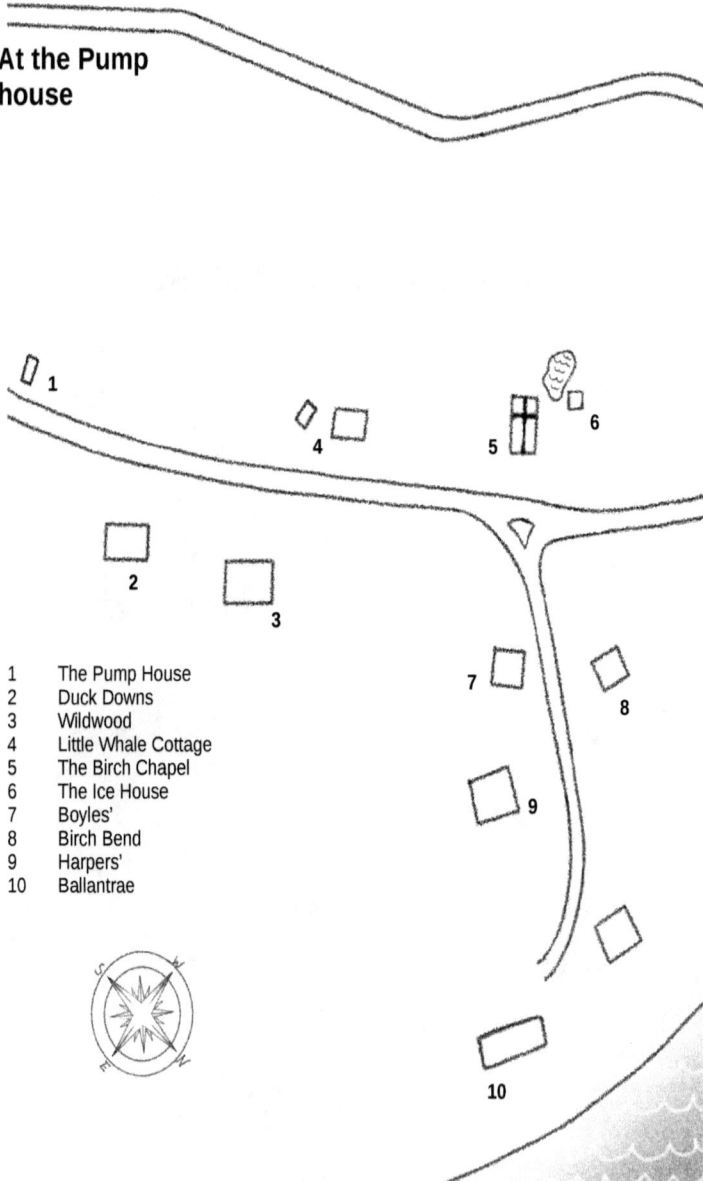

1   The Pump House
2   Duck Downs
3   Wildwood
4   Little Whale Cottage
5   The Birch Chapel
6   The Ice House
7   Boyles'
8   Birch Bend
9   Harpers'
10   Ballantrae

Duck Downs

124 Harbour View Road

The story of Duck Downs cottage and property began in the early 1980s, when Douglas Irvine purchased the land from his brother David and sister-in-law Sylvia. Lot #32, across from the pump house, was uphill from the late Hidden Hearth cottage, built in 1903 and owned by the Witherbee family. Unfortunately, that cottage was destroyed in a fire in 1965, caused by one of Flett's workers burning grass in the field.

The end of one cottage's life created a blank slate for a new beginning.

Nancy Irvine (Prescesky) had been coming to Smith's Cove from Montreal since she was three months old. Her parents owned The Prescesky Cottage (Lot #51), adding a familial layer to the already rich history of the area. Doug Irvine, the youngest brother of David, met Nancy through summer employment on the property and shared the dream of permanently relocating to Nova Scotia.

They planted their roots in 1980 when they were married in the

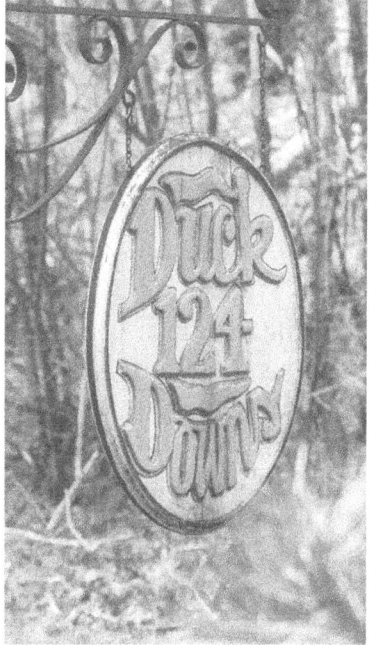

Birch Chapel.

With a resolute vision, Doug and Nancy embarked on the longest construction of a single private dwelling on the Harbou View property.

Doug Irvine working on Phase One

The initial phase commenced in the early 1980s, just before the birth of their first child, Dylan, in 1984. Nephew Marshall Webb worked with Doug to build a flat-roofed concrete foundation affectionately known as "Bunker One". It earned its nickname from nestling into the side of the hill ascending from Sulis Cove (commonly referred to as Smith's Cove). Every effort was made to incorporate materials from the property, such as a clawfoot bathtub, sinks, doors, and pine boards sourced from other cottages. Cedar shake shingles clad the exterior, connecting Duck Downs aesthetically with the surrounding cottages.

The landscape took shape around the summer dwelling through the integration of existing gardens. Nancy worked her magic in the gardens, tending to the old ones and crafting new ones with care. Her green thumb breathed fresh life into the landscape, weaving a blend of nostalgic charm and vibrant greenery as the summer dwelling expanded.

Doug, Nancy, and Dylan occupied the cottage during this phase. In 1990, they welcomed the birth of their second child, Nataleah.

Phase Two

As the Irvine family grew, phase two began and involved the expansion of the second foundation into the bank behind the first, providing much-needed bedrooms and amenities. A dynamic collaboration unfolded as Peter Hinton and Doug joined forces, infusing their creative workmanship into the expansion project The skilled hands of Marshall added an extra layer of craftsmanship, especially as he constructed the rounded deck that seamlessly connected the two foundations.

As the Irvines were both teachers, they spent their summers at Duck Downs, living amidst ongoing construction projects.

Phase Three

Phase three was initiated around November, 2010 and, over the next five to seven years, Eric Mombourquette contributed to the exquisite craftsmanship of the upstairs space. Doug, having recently retired, dedicated his time to working alongside Eric. Great consideration was devoted to the exterior design to preserve the architectural integrity of the community.

In 2018, Doug and Nancy moved upstairs, while Steve Mackin renovated the lower level ("Duck Downstairs") for Nataleah, Dylan, and their families.

The final version of Duck Downs, now equipped for year-round use, became a hub for family gatherings, vacations, and celebrations. Outdoor spaces evolved to accommodate the growing family, with various areas designed for different purposes and stages of life. The kitchen, strategically designed with prep spaces in mind, facilitated the cottage's role as a place for both large parties and cozy winter getaways.

2019: left to right, Greg and Nataleah (Irvine) Hanlon; Nancy and Doug Irvine; Jack, Meaghan and Dylan Irvine.

Every cottage at Harbour View, old or new, carries its own memories and traditions. The Irvines borrowed and contributed to these traditions, fostering a sense of community with fellow cottagers. Summertime "to do" lists (posted on the fridge) became a tradition: camping on Bear Island, weenie roasts and bonfires on the beach, boat rides, visiting Upper Clements Park, attending Good Times Day, Mavillette Beach picnics, and counting down the days until the annual Pool Party.

Duck Downs took approximately 38 years to complete, with Doug Irvine's premature death in November, 2020 marking the final chapter.

Despite the challenges of the COVID pandemic that year, Doug ensured the completion of the Zen Garden for Nataleah's wedding and the construction of Shed Two to house his cherished Kabota.

Doug's passion for the property extended to numerous projects, from rustic fencing to recovering preexisting stone walls and building sheds. His absence is felt, but his legacy lives on strongly in the completed structure.

In 2024, the cottage thrives and the Irvine family—spanning multiple generations—continues to be an integral part of the Harbour View community. Duck Downs stands as a testament to Doug's dedication, and he would undoubtedly be thrilled to see the place he envisioned continue to flourish.

Little Whale Cottage

141 Harbour View Road

The story of how Jim Sheridan and his family arrived in Smith's Cove begins around 1790, when Robert Snow was born in Liverpool England. It is not known exactly when, but Robert and his two brothers, all fishermen, decided to leave England for the new world.

Robert Snow, the eldest settled at Ecum Secum in Guysborough County. He died in 1891, age 100.

Robert Senior's son, William, born in 1830, was the first Snow to reside in Digby. He married Dorothy Greeley of Smith's Cove around 1852. Together they had eight children.

Their fourth son, later known as Captain William Snow, was born in 1865. Captain William married Blanche May Bent in 1898 and they had seven children.

Their fourth son, Vincent Snow, was born in 1912. He married Venetta Arnold of Kentville. In 1936 Vincent Snow started a shell fish processing and wholesaling business located on Digby's waterfront, which is now the Tidal Boat Works. Most of his product was exported to the USA and shipped to other provinces.

Vincent and Venetta had four children.

Their first daughter, Jean, was born in 1938. Jean married Harold Sheridan of Brockville, Ontario, whom she met at Mt. Allison University in New Brunswick.

Their son, Jim Sheridan, and his three siblings spent nearly every summer visiting family in the Digby area. Sometimes the family would travel by train from Ontario to spend time with their grandparents, Vincent and Venetta, at their home on Queen Street in Digby.

The small cottage

After a few years of renting cottages at Harbour View, Jim and his wife, Lisa, of Burlington, Ontario decided to build their own cottage at #141. In 2016 Little Whale Cottage was completed as a summer destination for Jim and Lisa and their three sons, Matthew, William and James.

Kevin McCully built a second small cottage in 2022 as the summer residence for Louis and Carol Puccini, Lisa's parents and resident pickleball enthusiasts. The late Kevin Hansen built the unique rustic wood shed west of the cottage.

Little Whale cottage is known for croquet on any sunny day, followed by blueberry picking in the patch behind the cottage. Old-fashioned cocktails and cigars on the porch sometimes appear after dark, and numerous Smith's Cove residents have become active members of the "The Tiny Cigar Club".

Jim and Lisa have recently purchased land west of the chapel for the enjoyment of future generations of Sheridans.

Wildwood

142 Harbour View Road

In 1996, the Hopgood family relocated to Toronto, where the children, Jane, Geoffrey and Sarah, completed their education. #77 Harbour View Road, the Hopgoods' "Linden Cottage", was sold; however, the love and nostalgia for the Harbour View Community was not discounted.

Approximately ten years later, Mary Ellen Hopgood returned with her guest, Frank McCrea, to a gracious welcome by all the residents of the property. It was a very positive initial introduction of the community for Frank. The following year, during a subsequent visit, Frank purchased #142 Harbour View Road from Russell

Fries.

The grounds and the building had been well tended; it had a most spectacular panoramic view of the Annapolis Basin, with a deep meadow in the foreground. The house itself possessed great character. The interior walls of the main room were defined by un-skinned vertical logs, a cathedral ceiling, an impressive beach-stone fireplace, and a quirky screen device for one half of the door to a long, wide, covered porch.

After reading Charles Turnbull's *The Harbour View Story* and *Historic Digby, Images of Our Past* by Mike Parker, Frank and Mary Ellen determined to limit their restoration of the cottage to making the building more comfortable, with very simple upgrades: kit-chen, bathroom, bedroom walls and floor refinishing, with the em-phasis on maintaining the original appearance of its 1910 heritage as much as possible.

The main room

Further to the history of this property, it was built in 1910 by the Dodds, of Massachusetts, then purchased by Miss Estelle Ogden of Boston in 1915. She and her devoted companion and cook summered there until Miss Ogden's death in 1938. One reads that she was friends of the Raymond family, and very fond of Kelsey Raymond, whose height she measured on the door post every year. The markings remain visible on the door frame of the entrance to the back porch.

Additionally, Miss Ogden was one of the principal benefactors of The Birch Chapel of St. Anne, referred to at Miss Ogden's time as "Church in the Wildwood." In addition to financial gifts, Miss Ogden donated the church bell and the organ.

Miss Simpson contributed to the pulpit and beautified the chapel with floral arrangements before the services.

In August, 2010, Geoff Hopgood introduced his long-time girlfriend, Lucy Dawson, to Harbour View. While they were playing scrabble one evening, he slipped an engagement ring into the bag of tiles. As a result, this cottage has a special place in their lives, later becoming the destination of their honeymoon.

In 2018 Lucy and Geoff and their children relocated from Toronto to Wolfville, Nova Scotia; they return to the cottage as often as possible with their three daughters, Penelope, Harriet and Olive, who now experience the enchantment.

Jane and Sarah Hopgood, and Frank and Mary Ellen, holiday there as much as possible. For all of us, the love for Harbour View and its community of friends grows with each visit.

The name "Wildwood" is chosen in recognition of Miss Ogden and Miss Simpson, their love for this cottage, Harbour View and their generous gifts to The Birch Chapel of St. Anne, "Church in the Wildwood."

The Birch Chapel

159 Harbour View Road

St. Anne's Birch Chapel continues to be a welcoming presence that hosts weddings, baptisms, and memorial services, as well as weekly Anglican services during July and August each year. The chapel is one of the diminishing number of places in Smith's Cove where locals and summer residents mingle, maintain friendships, and exchange news. Memorials to many departed friends and cottage community members hang on the walls.

In the winter of 2013-14, severe storms shifted the chapel off its foundations and put it out of action for the year. Members of the Harbour View community contributed over $16,000 to the work of preparing a new location for the chapel a little to the north of where it was originally, sinking sturdy new foundation posts, and moving the chapel onto them. The former location has become a parking area.

COVID-19 disrupted service schedules in 2020, but the chapel and its worshipping community are resilient and look forward to playing their part in Harbour View for a long time to come.

The Ice House

The ice house, with the sawdust pile on the right and Dave's chain saw in the foreground

Back in the Flett days, prior to 1967, all Harbour View rental cottages were equipped with an ice box that was supplied each day with property made ice. The ice was cut each winter on this pond located behind the Birch Chapel, stored in an ice house and covered with sawdust to keep it frozen well into the summer. Although the ice was traditionally cut with a special hand saw, David Irvine cut it with a chainsaw.

The winter of 1968 was very mild and the pond did not freeze to the normal thickness. As a result that was the last winter that ice was cut, and over the next few years all the cottages received electric refrigerators.

113

Boyles'

8 Chapel Lane

Russell Boyle often tells a story of the three most important things that he has done over his lifetime. He married Cathy, he bought a cottage, and he planted blueberry bushes. He is quick to note that these are not necessarily in order of importance.

One cannot always know the impact that our decisions in life can have. The purchase of the cottage at 8 Chapel Lane began a journey that has shaped the lives of the Boyle family. Harbour View became a place for rest, relaxation and retreat from the cares of life. The annual pilgrimage to it was much anticipated and so many fond memories were created there each summer.

The cottage has seen many changes and has housed lots of

friends and family over the 44 years of ownership by the Boyles. It started out as a quaint, two-bedroom abode with a tiny kitchen not much larger than a closet and a back yard that was covered in brambles and old bushes, and even a garbage pit from which were dug up a variety of old bottles used in the early 1900s. The cottage quickly became a home away from home for Cathy, Russ, Jen and Cindy.

The first addition to the cottage was in 1985, after the birth of Matthew. The front porch was enclosed, and side and front decks were added.

Russell and Cathy reclaimed the back yard and planted a small garden. Russell planted blueberry bushes and raspberry bushes and a small deck was added in that area.

Over the next few years, the family enjoyed every summer at Harbour View. Swimming in the pool, laughing on the tennis court, digging clams on the beach, running the trail and exercising at poolside took up much of their time. The kids renewed friendships each year and learned to swim and play tennis.

Cindy attended flower arranging classes with Mrs. Oliver and Jen and Cindy both worked in the kitchen at the hotel. Cathy learned to rug hook at the Smith's Cove Museum, where she was welcomed by many summertime friends, including Mary Lou Raymond, Nancy Conrad, Libby Morrell, Anna Hawkins and Juanita Soulis.

The love for Harbour View extended into the community as well. The summertime teas and Fireman's Breakfast and Fair are all cherished memories for the family. Part of the allure of Harbour View must include the community of Smith's Cove.

Cathy was encouraged to take up painting by Charles Turnbull and Frances Wetmore. Charles spent three hours in the blazing sun on the Boyles' deck one morning, painting beside Cathy. He was honing his craft through plein-air painting and was so generous in sharing his talent. Frances offered up her front deck and art expertise a few mornings a week. She and Charles organized a very successful art show at poolside.

Those times together chatting and painting will always be treasured and are a testament to the friendship and caring of the people at Harbour View.

That magical sense of well-being that comes over one as you crest the hill and drive under the last overpass on Highway 101 has been described by many. The skies could have been cloudy and gray during the entire drive, but it seems that there is always a line of cloud across the sky and then blue sky and Digby in the distance. It's a visceral experience that is difficult to describe, but seems to be a universal phenomenon for cottage owners and visitors alike. The Boyles' family and friends have often remarked on how peaceful and beautiful this area is.

The Boyle cottage has been a sanctuary for the family and for many friends. Among some of the annual visitors to the Boyle cottage are the Stitch and Bitch group that Cathy invites each year. You can hear their joyful laughter and music as they lounge on the deck and make trips into Frenchies and down to the French Shore. They have not tired of this vacation for 30 years and begin planning each year sometime in the spring, often just inquiring of Cathy, when would be a good date.

A large kitchen, fourth bedroom and covered side deck were added in 2006. More room was needed as the family grew.

Kiersten and Julia, the first grandchildren, quickly learned to love coming to the cottage. They joined in picking the blueberries and raspberries and always loved to make cottage pudding and thumbprint cookies with Nanny.

Russell would leave early each day with golf clubs and fishing rod in the trunk of the car. He would be gone most of the day, enjoying his favourite pastimes and would often bring home mackerel, which he would then distribute to cottagers and friends in the community.

The lot directly behind the cottage was purchased in the late 1990s and since that time a shed and bunkie have been added to the property. Russell's garden grew, and so did the family.

Jen married Jason in the Chapel in 2010. Cindy married Matt Foot. Their family grew to include Lauren and Fiona. Matt and Kate married, and their children, Vienna and Dominic, have already fallen in love with Harbour View. Kiersten and Jayden are parents of great-grandchildren, Kayden and Jackson.

Poolside is a riot of fun and laughter as these new generations on the property become friends, just as their parents did.

Harbour View was and always will be a place for healing, loving and friendship. It is a safe place where we can unwind from whatever life is throwing at us. It is a sanctuary for weary souls and a joyful retreat for relaxation and refueling. It has proven, indeed, to be one of the best things that Russ and Cathy have done in life; the family often talks about how lucky they are to have happened upon this magical place.

Figure 1: Cathy Boyle painting: 'Where's the booberries, Russell?'

Birch Bend

11 Chapel Lane

Built 1899. Argonaut Knoll's first building.

In 1997 Amanda Cox, her husband, Benjamin Bailey, and their two sons, Graham and Brent, made their first visit to Smith's Cove. The family was introduced to Harbour View by David and Suzie Turnbull. At that time, the Turnbulls and their three children were living in Charleston, West Virginia, where they were friends and neighbours of the Cox/Baileys.

The family rented Sylvia Harper's cottage, 20 Chapel Lane, their first summer. The subsequent two summers they stayed at "Pioneer Cabin", 11 Chapel Lane, which was owned by Sylvia Harper's four children. In 2000, the Cox/Baileys bought the cottage from them. Several years later they renamed it "Birch Bend" because of the birch tree that once grew alongside the unusual curved deck, built by Marshall Webb for the Harpers in the 1990s.

Memorable to all were treks to Bear Island, dressing up to go to the Harbour View Inn for luscious dinners and legendary slices of mud pie. Beach fires, the Cottagers' Association pool party, tennis tournaments, and picnics made summers rich in everlasting friendships, thus strengthening the family's ties to Nova Scotia and this unique community.

Amanda, Graham and Brent were also taught how to hook by the "hookers" during their weekly gatherings at the Smith's Cove Museum. St. Anne's Birch Chapel, within sight of the cottage, has provided a place of quiet reflection and contemplation, season after season.

Forays outside Harbour View to Bear River included stops at "The Leopard-Skin Pillbox-Hat", a vintage shop, long gone, where treasures and curiosities of all kinds could be found. Many summers the family went to Beartown Baskets in the Mi'kma'ki Community to watch Chief Greg McEwan make traditionally-woven baskets with beautiful-carved ash handles.

In 2023 major renovations were made to Birch Bend. A small room was built out onto the deck at the front of the cottage. This allowed for the installation of a new kitchen opening into the living room.

The space now includes a pantry and eat-in dining area.

The original kitchen was in the back corner of the cottage and had not been updated since the 1970s. A laundry room and additional storage have taken its place.

Larger doors and windows were installed throughout, adding light, a sense of spaciousness and expanding views of the Annapolis Basin and Bear Island.

In an effort to maintain the character of this 1899 structure, the original stone fireplace and flooring were left in place. The unfinished walls have been faced with tongue and groove panelling. A stand up shower and new sink were installed in the bathroom, but the clawfoot tub remains.

To the exterior, a new roof, gutters, downspouts and lighting were added, as well new cedar shakes. Horizontal whole logs, dating from when Charles F. Chase had the cabin built, frame the area below the front roofline and door.

Harpers'

20 Cottage Lane

Note Cole and Jermay on the roof, 2023

Donald Harper and Daisy Fitch (née Harper) are first cousins. Daisy's mother Tiffin (widow of Raymond Harper) married Allen Shenstone and subsequently was introduced to Harbour View. Daisy suggested the Harper family vacation there and so in 1974 they did for the first time.

All parties instantly agreed this was paradise and the place they wanted to be every summer.

The Harpers rented various cottages over the years, but the fantastic, birch two-story house owned by the Shenstones was their favourite.

In 1986, they were able to purchase #42 Harbour View Road, what is now #20 Chapel Lane. Sylvia became the sole owner of the cottage after she and Donald divorced in the 1990s.

In 2017, the four Harper 'children': **Anne, Malcolm, Claire, and**

Jeanne, who all live in Massachusetts, became trustees of the cottage. Their goal is to preserve and protect the cottage for future generations, which include Malcolm's daughters Chloe and Hannah Harper, Claire's sons Linden and Jeramy Adamson, and Jeanne's sons Cole and Leo Hennen.

In 1986 the cottage was not in good shape. The first order of business was to hire a mason to repair the eroded support for the brick chimney, which was about to collapse. Then David Irvine was hired to stabilize the interior of the cottage. He also created a proper kitchen (there was simply a hot plate in a tiny nook) and added cupboards, a stove, and a hot water heater.

Over the years, Sylvia envisioned and oversaw many improvements. The exterior went from an unfriendly dark brown to the soft gray of aged cedar. To help with storage, a large shelf was built high on the wall in the kitchen, becoming a loft for suitcases, bicycles, and the like. A few years later, a second bathroom was added, with room for a washer and dryer.

A wood stove was installed in the kitchen to provide heat in the shoulder seasons. Then a spacious sunny bedroom with closets and bookshelves was built on the southeast side of the building.

122

Originally, a covered porch spanned the length of the water side of the cottage. This feature made for a dim, cramped interior and somewhat disconnected the inside from the view of Annapolis Basin. So Sylvia's final improvement project was to enlarge the living/dining room by enclosing a large portion of the front porch. The front wall was pushed out and filled with windows. This created a spacious, light filled, welcoming interior without changing the footprint of the building and, importantly, made the gorgeous view a primary focus.

Sylvia, a fine gardener, hired a backhoe to remove the hard, rocky ground and replace it with nourishing soil. Along the road, she planted a smoke bush and a hedge of lilacs and hydrangeas. On the southeast side of the cabin, she planted white birches and created an area for blueberries and perennials. As the blueberries became established, neighbour Russell Boyle kindly applied his special fertilizer each May. The Harpers love having fresh-picked blueberries with breakfast, and flowers on the table.

The Harpers have shared countless wonderful times at the cottage. From delicious meals of fresh specialties from places like Annapolis Farmers Market, to endless games and creative projects, to reading books, and enjoying long chats in front of the fire. They've been serenaded by distant cries of loons and seagulls and entranced by the ever-changing tide, sky, and stars.

2024 marks 50 years at Harbour View for the Harper family. One of the things they have liked best is that, so far, four generations of family have basked in its beauty and warmth.

Claire Harper's recollections, with contributions from Jeanne Harper

Claire has very fond memories of her childhood summer vacations at Smiths Cove. She got to know other kids by playing Duck-Duck-Goose and other fun games at the children's program in Cossaboom Corner. David and Sylvia Irvine rented out horses, Flash and Queenie, and a pony named Smokey. The children rode around the property, and the unflappable Smokey was Claire's favourite.

The now-buried blue cement pool was the centrepiece of fun, where adults gabbed and kids dove, flipped, and did cannonballs off the diving board. Teenaged Marshall Webb staged concerts poolside, singing the fan favourite about Smokey's farts with his younger siblings and their Irvine cousins.

The beach, Bear Island, and the Annapolis Basin offered tons of fun. All ages sailed together on Saturday-morning (stiff breezes) and Wednesday-night (often becalmed) sailboat races. The community moored their sailboats in deeper water, but the boats still sat on the mud flats at low tide.

Skiffs were anchored on the pebble beach, and kids used them to fish for flounder or row to Bear Island. At night, they whittled skewers and roasted marshmallows over beach bonfires under the stars. Teens sometimes spent the night on Bear Island, wearing their Frenchy's finest, and everyone at Harbour View knew because the seagulls protested incessantly.

Get-togethers with family and friends were memorable affairs. Great-aunt Tiffin and Allen Shenstone's union blended three generations of Harpers and Shenstones. They wore bibs for lobster feasts and dressed up for cocktail parties. There were road trips, sometimes *en masse*, and yearly visits to Brier Island as they explored Nova Scotia.

Looking back over the last fifty years, the warm and welcoming community is always the best part—as steadfast and lovely as the 23-28-foot tide that rises and falls without fail in the Annapolis Basin.

Ballantrae

Soon to be 'Tigh Na Mara' (House by the Sea)
34 Chapel Lane

Harbour View, Smith's Cove, Nova Scotia, Canada...an address that mystified and fascinated Priscilla Squiers as a child when she would write to her grandmother, Helen Odell Squiers, each summer. From the photos she'd seen, Harbour View seemed like an enchanted locale exuding an otherworldly light; Helen's piercing blue eyes were matched by the brilliant hue of the sky and the Annapolis Basin.

In her letters, Helen regaled us with stories of her time with friends, competitive bridge games, reading on the porch, and arranging her favourite. flowers. Priscilla was intrigued. What was this place?

Priscilla's parents, James (Jim) and Virginia (Jinnie) Squiers, had history at Harbour View as well. They had both summered at Smith's Cove as children. Jim; his parents, John and Helen; aunt and uncle, Van and Eliott Odell; first cousin, Lynn Odell; and grandparents, Louise Dade and Rev. Charles Frederick Odell, all spent time at Seagull Cottage. Jinnie and her parents, Caswell and Virginia Milbank Barrie, stayed in what is now Cormore Cottage. Jinnie's Milbank cousins also came up to visit, so family was never far away in those early days.

As adults, Jim and Jinnie were interested in vacationing in other places. They eventually retired from Connecticut to Sarasota, Florida, but their love for Harbour View was rekindled when they decided on a whim to visit Smith's Cove in the early 1980s. They were smitten.

As kismet would have it, the Englehart cottage next to the Odell cottage became available, and Jim and Jinnie became homeowners. They called their new abode Ballantrae, which had also been the name of Caswell Barrie's prize-winning Scottish Terrier kennels in Scarsdale, NY many years before.

The family, 1981

With David Irvine's impeccable expertise and hard work, Jim and Jinnie enlarged and winterized Ballantrae, putting in a full kitchen and a larger primary bedroom on the main level, and making a cozy den out of the original bedroom. On the lower level, they created an apartment-style living space with a small kitchen, living area, bedroom and bath, and added a garage.

The 1980s and early 90s were golden years in Nova Scotia for Priscilla's parents. Jim and Jinnie enjoyed summer gatherings and the warm friendship of the community. Jinnie loved entering flower arrangements in the Digby Pines Flower Show, searching for second-hand treasures at Frenchy's, and attending the Weymouth Tea with friends. Jim adored sailing with Kelsey Raymond, singing in the local church choir, and devouring as many books as he could while sunning himself on the deck and enjoying a cigar.

As they became less fond of Florida life, Jim and Jinnie extended their time at Ballantrae into the winter months, parking their GMC Jimmy at the top of the hill by the Harpers' cottage when the drive was icy and gamely making their way down to the house. They relished the good humour of progressive dinners, competitive card nights, walks with their dachshunds, and the satisfaction of fully stocking their chest freezer.

Priscilla started coming up regularly in the early 1980s. She and her husband, Kyle Minor, flew up from Connecticut for Christmas with her parents on several occasions, and enjoyed cross country skiing in the pristine snow around the Harbour View property and in Bear River.

As their family grew, Priscilla and Kyle introduced their children to Harbour View during yearly summer visits with Kieran (b. 1996), Olivia (b. 2002), and twins Arden and Viola (b. 2006). They would stay at Ballantrae and next door at Cousin Lynn's Seagull Cottage.

Favourite family haunts included Upper Clements Theme Park (the log flume being a favourite.), the Wildlife Park, the Habitation, Summerville Beach on the South Shore, and Digby Neck and the Islands. In more recent years, the young adults have savoured their camping trips in Keji and Blomidon.

Kieran and Arden enjoying cottage life, 2016

Although poor health prevented her parents from returning to Ballantrae in their final years, Priscilla and Kyle are convinced that Jim and Jinnie found their Eden during the almost 30 years they lived in Harbour View. During this time, Jinnie valiantly battled cancer and heart disease and endured disfiguring surgeries, but always felt renewed when she returned to her beloved home in Smith's Cove.

As it has been for many families past and present, Harbour View is special in so many ways: it heals, restores and reconnects us. Case in point: In 1997, Jinnie suffered septic shock and was rushed up to Kentville, where she was given a 10% chance of survival. When Priscilla arrived at the hospital, she was happily surprised to be greeted by her former Bowdoin classmate, Lynne Harrigan, who was one of the ER physicians at Kentville.

Jinnie was in good hands, and soon, both she and Jim were back home in Smith's Cove, looking out at the amazing blue of the sky and the Annapolis Basin. Kismet indeed.

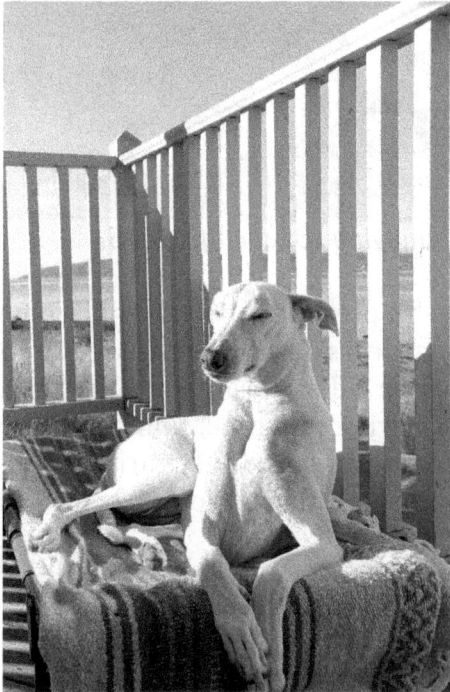

Wiggles holding court on the deck

Past the chapel

Past the chapel

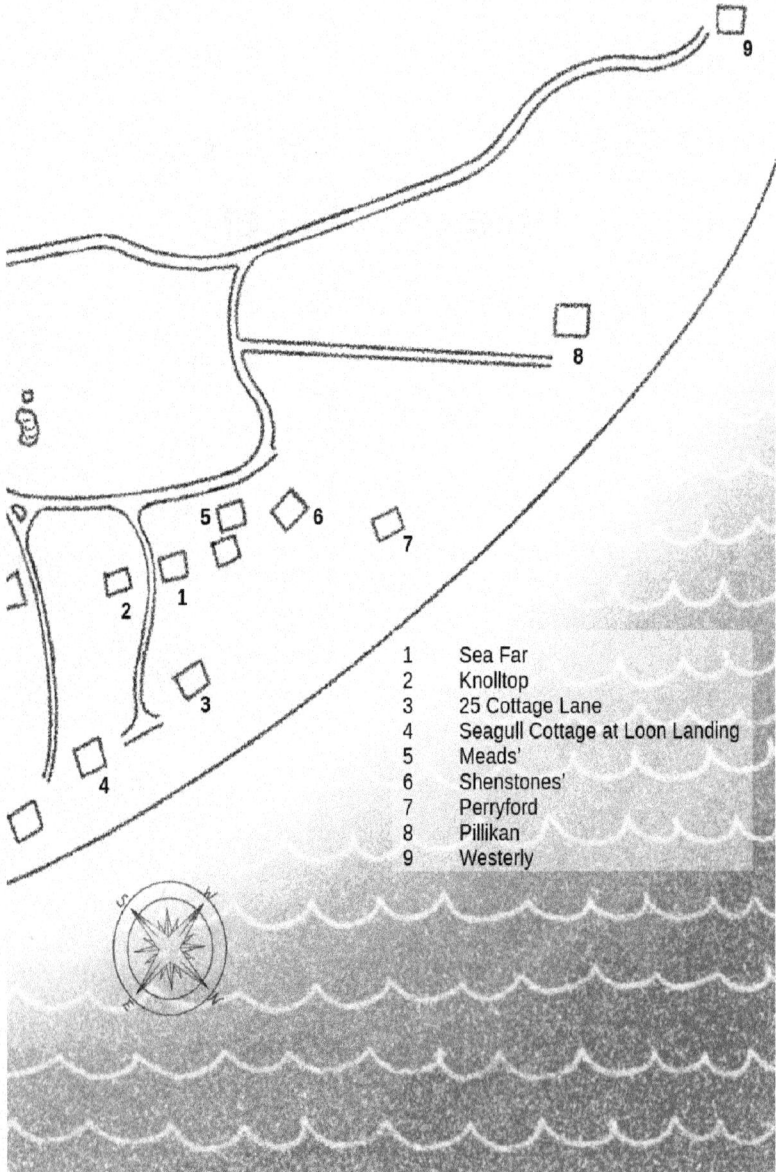

1	Sea Far
2	Knolltop
3	25 Cottage Lane
4	Seagull Cottage at Loon Landing
5	Meads'
6	Shenstones'
7	Perryford
8	Pillikan
9	Westerly

Sea Far

5 Cottage Lane

In 1996, ownership of the cottage, named affectionately as Sea Far Cottage by Mrs Rhu, was transferred to her daughter, Barbara Wilkins.

Barbara, the sister of Hugh Smith, has vacationed at Harbour View since early childhood. St. Anne's Chapel has been the site of many fond memories for the Wilkins family as the church where Barbara married James Wilkins of Calgary and where their first-born son was christened and married.

The entire roof of the cottage was removed in 2016 as part of major renovations undertaken by Kevin McCully. These renovations included additional space, pine interior walls and ceilings and a beautiful screened-in porch from which to enjoy Harbour View's spectacular waters and sunrises.

The original fireplace from 1903 remains to this day.

Knolltop

6 Cottage Lane

The original Knoll Top, around 1909

In 1909, guests at 'Knoll Top'—a two-story hotel of log construction on Argonaut Knoll—sat on the hotel's veranda and savoured the magnificent, panoramic beauty of the Annapolis Basin, a vista that stretched from Digby Gut to the mouth of the Bear River.

More than a hundred years later, the Rev. and Mrs. Mike (Donna) Coram, joined by family and friends, savoured the same magnificent view each summer from the front deck of their cottage on the site where the hotel once stood.

Perhaps, the Corams often mused, long before there was a log hotel on Argonaut Hill, Mi'kmaq families savoured the same view from their summer fishing encampments on this spot.

After the hotel was torn down in the 1930s, a small cottage was built around the hotel's remaining mammoth stone fireplace in the 1940s.

The Corams bought the cottage in 1978 and named it 'Knolltop'. They celebrated with a house blessing in 1980, inviting the Harbour View community to participate and to enjoy a wine and cheese party on their front deck.

Knolltop now.

'Knolltop' is a modest, two-bedroom, insulated cottage—cool and comfortable in hot weather; warm and cozy in chilly weather.

Through the years, encroaching forests around the cottage were removed and replaced by expansive green lawns, seven flower beds, and privacy fencing. In 2001, the 1909 stone fireplace needed costly repairs. It was removed and replaced by a brick fireplace and chimney.

After Charles F. Chase purchased the land he called Argonaut Knoll, around 1899, he advertised 'Knoll Top' hotel as a spot for rest and recuperation for 'mind, body, and nerves'. The Corams, too, have found it the spot to feel cheered and renewed, refreshed and made whole.

Mike Coram often said that it was the place where he clearly saw the hand of the Creator, and not the hand of man.

In 2019, Mike passed away. A wall plaque in his memory is inside St. Anne's (the Birch Chapel). The plaque was blessed during the Sunday morning Eucharist on July 9, 2023. It reads:

The Reverend Jame Michael (Mike) Coram
1939-2019
Now thank we all our God,
whose hand created the beauty of sky, land and sea;
and who gave the gift of many happy summers at Harbourview,
amidst His glorious creation.
A loving remembrance by
Donna G. Coram,
wife

REST

To look out over a broad expanse of natural scenery is always restful. The panoramic view shown in this folder was taken from the roof of Pioneer Cabin on Argonaut Knoll. For beauty and variety it cannot be excelled anywhere in the world.

When you realize that Digby Gut is seven miles away and Bear Island one mile you can readily appreciate that as your eye looks out upon such scenery there is rest for your mind body and nerves.

Several years ago we came seeking a place where we could have a good wholesome vacation without "fuss and feathers" and without much expense.

We found it at Smith's Cove a little village midway between Digby and Bear River Nova Scotia. The air was fresh delightfully cool and invigorating. Excursions by land and water to points of interest were of almost daily occurrence and very reasonable.

The facilities for bathing boating fishing driving tennis and the absence of mosquitoes led us to purchase Argonaut Knoll and build Pioneer Cabin. In it we have already spent a number of happy summers.

The cosy cabin with its complete equipment and picturesque surroundings brought forth so many favorable comments from our visitors we built other cabins for rent.

Parties of from four to twelve can rent a whole cabin or single rooms may be engaged in Knoll Top, a large two story cabin. Every cabin is completely furnished including bed linen blankets and small oil stove.

In each cabin's ample living room a large fire place bids defiance to storm and chill.

A telephone on the Knoll provides instant communication with telegraph office and good physicians at Bear River and Digby.

A forty foot drive well supplies each cabin with an abundance of sparkling running water.

For six dollars ($6) per week you can get well cooked wholesome and nicely served meals at the Harbor View House nearby at the end of a winding woodland walk. Teams are provided without extra cost for those who prefer to ride.

Argonaut Knoll is a trifle over a mile from Bear River Station Dominion Atlantic Ry. Steamers run daily from Boston and semi-weekly from New York. If you are interested to learn more address

Telephone Connection   CHAS F CHASE 39-41 Cortlandt St New York City

Charles Chase's advertisement for Knoll Top

25 Cottage Lane

Tiffin Shenstone died in 1987, at which time her surviving daughter, Daisy Fitch, took possession of the cottage. See the entry for the Mead property.

Daisy made a number of significant renovations to the cottage, contracting John Postma for the majority of the work.

First the deck was expanded to afford more outdoor gathering space, and stairs were built to create direct access to the beach. The kitchen was remodelled to include the creation of an adjacent sitting room, built out over the footprint of the former covered patio.

This was followed by redesigning the master bedroom and bath. The intention was to open the cottage to the stunning views of the Basin, Bear Island and the Gut, much beloved by Daisy, who always declared this view "the best." A new roof was installed in 2020, and most recently the original fireplace and chimney, badly in need of repair, were replaced during the off-season in 2022-23. At the same time a mini-split was added to increase comfort during the early and late season months, as well as to combat the warmer summers the planet has been increasingly experiencing.

Daisy was an attentive gardener and could often be found weeding the abundant perennial beds originally installed by Rita Mathers; further developed by Tiffin Shenstone. Val Fitch died in February 2015, and Daisy in February 2024, just a few weeks shy of her 90th birthday. Daisy leaves the legacy of her deep love for Harbour View and the Cove, as well as her beloved cottage to her three children, Locke Harvey, Douglas Wilkinson, and MacKenzie Sharp.

Daisy Fitch revelling in her garden

Seagull Cottage at Loon Landing

28 Cottage Lane

In the early 1900s, Louise Dade Odell, Lynn's grandmother, was invited by Reverend Melendez to visit Smith's Cove. It was love at first sight, and that affection (addiction may be closer to the truth) has passed on to each succeeding generation of Odell.

Behind the lilacs on the front porch and across the rugosa rose hedge is the residence of the late Jim Squiers, Lynn's first cousin and son of Lynn's beloved aunt, Helen Odell Squiers, and his lovely "bride" Jinnie, also now deceased. Their daughter, Priscilla Squiers, her husband, Kyle Minor, and their family now own the cottage.

It is said that Lynn's English grandmother was attracted to the Cove because of its close resemblance to the area of Scotland where she spent her summers as a child. Lynn feels there is a more mystical basis to the family connection.

It is hard to believe that it was mere coincidence that led Lynn's grandmother to build a cottage in same community where Loyalist Odells fled to escape persecution during the American Revolution —this fact not discovered until the late 1950s. Or that she just happened to select a piece of property that was, in 1792, deeded by King George III, along with the fishing rights, to an ancestor, Daniel Odell. This last tidbit not revealed until 1991!

The grant of fishing rights from King George III

The cottage was built in 1916 by Ralph Cositt, who built most of the older cottages on the property as well as the Birch Chapel (St. Anne's) on the top of the hill. Lynn's grandmother, like the rest of the original cottage owners, was unable to purchase the land on which their cottages stood. They held ninety-nine year leases. Lynn's grandmother's lease would have expired in the year 2015!

At that time, Harbour View House and Cottages was quite a fashionable (albeit rustic) place to summer.

The Harbour View property is much the same as it was 100 years ago—only a few modifications here and there. In the early years, there was shed in front of the barn that housed some of the residents' limousines. High tea was the major social event of the day and the clothing protocol required "whites" on both the tennis and croquet courts.

The lease agreement required cottage owners to pay for meals at the main dining room at the Inn—now the "motel" section—whether they ate there or not. As a result, none of the original cottages were built with kitchens.

The "breakfast room" in the cottage was originally an open back porch (therefore the shingles on the inside walls). The kitchen area consisted of one small sink, an ice box (yes, with ice delivered several times a week) followed by a very small refrigerator which Lynn's father, Elliot Odell, turned into a freezer (its sole function being to make ice cubes for the "happy hour"), and a two-burner hot plate.

In many ways Lynn will always miss the command performances in the main dining room of the Inn, now converted into four guest rooms. It gave all the cottage dwellers, both renters and private owners, the opportunity to gather together at least once a day.

The scene was rarely dull. The breakfast ritual included an open debate carried on across the dining room on the weather forecast for the day, the tide schedule and, more often than not, who would be the crew for an outing on "Admiral" Allen Shenstone's Lightning[1]. Upon the death of Dr. Shenstone, the command of the Basin fleet passed on to Admiral Kelsey Raymond. Kelsey died in 2000 and no new Admiral has been named.

Invariably there was a happy hour before dinner, which rotated

---

1   The oldest sailboat of its class still afloat.

from cottage to cottage. At the same magical moment each evening, a caravan of cars would wend its way down the road and, much to the distress of the waitresses and fascination of the Inn's guests, deposit anywhere from 10 to 20 happy souls in the dining room.

For each reserved table (regular Harbourviewites had the same table year after year), there are numerous stories to be told. At the Odell table, the warfare between Lynn's father, Eliott, and his sister, Helen, is legendary. For years a secret lottery was held, the lucky winner having determined at which point during dinner Lynn's father would have so aggravated Lynn's aunt that she would storm out of the dining room and walk back to the cottage at sufficient pace to raise dust on the road.

The Harbour View community owes David and Sylvia Irvine a tremendous debt of gratitude for the fact that little has changed on the property over the years. In the late 1960s, they bought the property and quickly set about selling the private owners the land on which their cottages stood. David modernized and then sold the rental cottages. Now all cottages on the property are privately owned.

Seagull Cottage kept pace (slow) with the modernization. The original footed bathtub and wooden toilet seat in the cottage were replaced (to Lynn's never-ending distress) by the modern ac-coutrements now found in the cottage bathroom (actually they may be not be considered "modern" at this point). The garage (rarely ever used as such) was transformed (by master builder David Irvine) into HOSA (Helen Odell Squiers Annex).

More recent years brought the first serious refrigerator and, in 1988, a renovated kitchen, rebuilt front porch, and, joy of joys, a septic system. Lynn won't describe the previous waste disposal system. Let it suffice to say that it was as primitive as they come.

"Seagull" was the original name of the cottage. Because Lynn considers herself a little dotty on the subject of loons (as in the oldest species of bird) and because of their faithful appearance each year in front of the cottage at certain tides, she decided a number of years ago to tack on "Loon Landing" thereby creating

"SEAGULL COTTAGE at Loon Landing".

Lynn's first trip up was when she was 3 so that would have been 1947. There were so few trees on the property that when her mother wanted Lynn to come home for dinner she would hang a red towel on their porch and Lynn could see it from the pool.

Another story was of sitting in the back of a horse-drawn wagon with ice being delivered. Each of the cottages needed ice to keep their food fresh in the ice box. The cart was also used to collect corn and tomatoes. She and Hugh Smith would sit in the back of the truck and eat the tomatoes before they were delivered. Many children on the property were also drawn to the frog pond behind the chapel as another activity.

One of her earliest memories was that she wanted to go sailing. Admiral Shenstone promised he would take her when she got her certificate for swimming and when she got it, she couldn't even talk, she was so excited. She just held up the certificate and he took her sailing.

Mary Lou Raymond was the waitress at the Inn and Lynn would go down to talk to her or just spend time with her. It was the basis of a long and loving relationship of sailing, visiting or having dinner together.

Lynn repeatedly told a story about Molly and Admiral Shenstone going to see a big event at the base. Molly was a big woman and when she met the head of the event she said something about not being able to sit on the grass. When they arrived for the event there were two overstuffed chairs on the lawn with Admiral Shenstone's name on one and Molly Shenstone's on the other.

Lynn would go to Nova Scotia with her Aunt Helen during her school and teenage years. Lynn attended Camp Arcadie during the summer. The girls would periodically sneak out over the road to a nearby boys' camp. One of the girls had a head injury and they stopped that.

Lynn starred as the modern major general in *Pirates of Penzance* at camp. Aunt Helen rented a car to attend every performance. During cold and rainy days Lynn and Aunt Helen would play Scrabble near the fireplace and switch places to get the other side of their bodies warm near the fire.

When Lynn's dad died and Lynn inherited the cottage, Lynn would have parties with her friends and Aunt Helen would rest up at HOSA (Helen Odell Squires Annex) while the party raged on till all hours. Aunt Helen would never sleep up in the Annex. She wanted what she considered "her bed". At the end of the party, Lynn would sometimes have to wake Aunt Helen and Aunt Helen would then come down to sleep in the cottage.

Aunt Helen snored and Lynn would have trouble getting to sleep so she would try her darnedest to get to sleep before Aunt Helen, who evidently shook the walls with her snoring. If that didn't work she would bang on the wall and Aunt Helen would stop for a bit and Lynn would try again to get to sleep before Aunt Helen.

Memorial Day in the States is a three-day weekend at the end of May. Lynn and a couple of friends would extend the three days to five. By catching the ferry from Portland, Maine on Thursday night the group, could arrive Friday morning in Yarmouth and make the short drive to Smith's Cove. The cottage would be a hive of activity, unloading duty-free rum from the car, arranging flowers, and getting out Lynn's favourite things that had been put away for the winter.

Everything had its proper place. One year Ellen deliberately faced a ceramic loon in the 'wrong' direction. Lynn looked perplexed for a moment, then made the correction. Ellen did it again, Lynn turned it the right way—again. On the third go-round, Lynn was not amused, announced that it was "just wrong" as she turned it to the 'correct' position and went off in a huff while the helpers burst out laughing.

With everything in its correct place, we could have a nap before the evening party began.

Meads'

184 Harbour View Road

The Mead property runs alongside the Shenstone property to its west, and drops down to what is now the Fitch property at its eastern corner.

The three estates and their families share a history going back to the summer of 1969, when widow and pianist Tiffin Harper came to Smith's Cove to marry widower and physicist Allen Shenstone in the Birch Chapel on 22 August. The Shenstone family had owned property at Harbour View since 1906-1908, but its cottage was destined for Michael Shenstone, Allen's son by his first marriage.

Wanting a place where she and Allen could continue summering in Smith's Cove, Tiffin Shenstone bought the adjacent Lot 24 from

Harbour View House and Cottages Limited in 1973.

Cottage #47, the historic cabin on this plot of land, dates to 1903. Once approached by a road from below, it sits near the top of a roughly rectangular parcel that falls away from Harbour View Road, descending north to the cliff and shoreline that overlook the Annapolis Basin and Bear Island. The cabin was built by Harbour View House for summer guests who slept here while taking their meals at the hotel. Anchored by a monumental fireplace of field-stone, the cabin was venerable but primitive, with dark rooms, minimal views, and scant facilities.

Tiffin wanted something more comfortable and more open to the land and seascape. She turned to William Shellman, an archi-tect she knew from Princeton, New Jersey, where she and Allen lived during the year. Bill came up for a visit in the summer of 1974 and, over the months of July and August, drew up a gabled 'Cottage for Dr. and Mrs. Allen Shenstone'. Set toward the bottom of the lot, the evolving design for the cottage embraced the views and light with generous windows and a plan whose spaces flowed out from the interior rooms to an exterior sun trap and porch.

The project came to an abrupt halt in the fall of 1974, after Rita Mathers decided to sell her cottage just to the east along the shore. As she explained that October in a letter to Dave Irvine, "I let Mrs. Shenstone know about it—as I promised her I would...she bought it 'as is'—and intends to take it over in June."

Unlike the rustic cabin, the Mathers Cottage was a modern dwelling from the 1950s, came fully furnished, and had a well-ten-ded garden.

Tiffin transferred ownership of both properties to her daugh-ters, art historian Katherine Mead and the journalist Daisy Sharp—on the understanding that she and Allen would summer in the former Mathers Cottage, as they did until his death in 1980 and her death in 1987.

Katherine and Daisy took on Cottage #47, and incrementally turned what they called the Little Cabin into a habitable vacation home. Improvements—carried out by Dave Irvine during the off seasons—included new and enlarged bedroom windows, a skylight in the living room, a new and complete kitchen in the back, a second bathroom, extensions to the deck outside, and a concrete foundation for the fireplace, which was tilting dangerously as it settled into the ground.

In 1983, Katherine died with tragic suddenness in an automobile accident. Her share of the two properties passed to her sons, Christopher and Lawrence Mead, who became co-owners of the Little Cabin in partnership with their Aunt Daisy.

Though Katherine's death was devastating for everyone in her family, it proved particularly cruel for Tiffin and contributed to her suicide in 1987; mother and daughter now rest side-by-side in the Smith-Sulis Cemetery at Harbour View.

Daisy Fitch—she had married the physicist Val Fitch in 1976—settled into her mother's cottage, and her nephews got the cabin up the hill, a pragmatic arrangement that was codified when the Fitch property and the Mead property were legally separated in 1990.

Christopher and his wife, Michele Penhall, and Lawrence and his wife, Trish Walter, live far from Nova Scotia, in Albuquerque, New Mexico, and all were busy at the time with their careers: Christopher as a professor, department chair, and later college dean; Michele as a doctoral student and then museum curator; Lawrence as a practising architect; Trish as an administrative assistant, among other jobs. Their visits to Smith's Cove tended to be harried and brief, barely long enough to catch their breath before rushing back home.

But as the 1990s headed into the next century, Christopher and Michele began to prepare for their eventual retirement and the promise of more time at Harbour View. To obviate the difficulties that attend co-tenancy—the strain of scheduling visits, supervising maintenance, settling bills—Christopher revived his grandmother's project for a modern cottage on the property.

The Little Cabin went to Lawrence, along with the liberty to alter it as he wished, while Christopher would build a second dwelling at his own expense.

Christopher sketched the preliminary design in July 2004. Over a week of solid rain, huddled by the fireplace against the Little Cabin's cold and damp, he and Michele drew up the program of practical needs and aspirational desires that shaped a compact shelter 30 feet on a side. The original concept did not change, despite the refinements introduced over the next three years of design development—and budgeting—that produced the final plans in December 2007.

To accommodate two structures, Christopher had the property resurveyed in 2004 and replaced the existing, rudimentary cesspit with a modern septic system in 2007.

The new cottage was built by the carpenter John Postma, working in stages during the off-seasons from the Fall of 2008 to the Spring of 2014.

After Christopher retired in 2013, joined a year later by Michele, they could finally spend more time at Harbour View.

The cottage adopts the local vernacular of timber-framed construction sheathed with cedar shingles. But it also reflects Christopher's interests as a historian and professor of architecture. In plan, the cottage is a rotated square, inspired by villas of the Italian architect Andrea Palladio, and houses by American architect Louis Kahn and Japanese architect Kazuo Shinohara.

Organized along a diagonal axis cut across the square, the interior leads from its main entrance at the rear south corner through a hallway to a square great room at the opposite north corner. This great room combines a kitchen island with areas for living, dining, and entertainment, and it faces east and west toward the views and breezes through tall sliding glass doors that flank a free-standing Malm fireplace in the corner.

Symmetrical bedroom suites with clothes closets and bathrooms occupy the east and west corners of the cottage to either side of the great room. The roof mirrors the plan's spatial geometry by folding the square along the diagonal to form two triangles that climb from eaves at nine feet along the back to a peak of 18 feet at the front north corner.

The structure applies lessons from Shinohara and traditional Japanese architecture, with rafters set at 45° to the diagonal supports of two microlam beams over the great room.

The cottage answers to the interdependent constraints and advantages of its site. Property setbacks, code requirements, and simple common sense prevented a usable footprint of space between the Little Cabin and the Wilkins cottage to the immediate southeast—and would have meant cutting down two mature Scotch pines planted there by Dave Irvine in 1990. This pushed the cottage farther down, nestled toward the eastern property line to avoid blocking the basin view from Lawrence's cabin while staying above the septic drainage field that traverses the lot at an angle from west to east. These restrictions put the cottage at a topographic edge where the lot drops steeply toward the water from its flat upper section.

The south entrance starts at ground level but, from there, the structure floats into space, hoisted on hemlock piers that stand at 5-8 feet beneath the great room and reach 9-12 feet beneath the outdoor deck that propels the cottage deeper into the view.

The cottage orients south to north for both climatic and aesthetic reasons. Screened by its roof from the daily southern arc of strong sunlight in summer, the interior turns toward the diffused northern light preferred by artists. Simultaneously, the sliding glass doors in the great room capture the breezes that rise naturally up the hillside from the Annapolis Basin, cooling the cottage in a sustainable cycle whose benefits become increasingly obvious in our age of global warming. And the deck surveys a panoramic sweep of land and water from Digby Gut to the Annapolis Basin and Bear River.

Between 2017 and 2023 (interrupted by the pandemic), Christopher crafted a teahouse at the approximate place where his grandmother had planned her cottage four decades earlier. The Japanese teahouse is an idealized home and follows strict protocols that detail its parts, spaces, and rituals. Yet, paradoxically, these never dictate its final form. Every teahouse is unique, because each adapts a tradition going back five centuries to present conditions of where, when, and by whom it is created.

Every teahouse is founded as well on an ethic of poverty and simplicity called *wabi sabi*, which stipulates that it be made primarily from humble local materials: things available at the local hardware store, in other words, not imported from Japan.

A Japanese teahouse becomes a Nova Scotian teahouse in Smith's Cove. Canadian cedar shingles replace Japanese clay walls, porch columns and tearoom fixtures use a spruce tree cut down on the property, white plexiglass panels replace sliding screens of rice paper (*shōji*), polycarbonate panels replace a roof of reed thatch. The bamboo roof rafters are Japanese in spirit but were cultivated at Christopher's home in Albuquerque and commemorate the migration of his teahouse from Japan to Nova Scotia by way of New Mexico.

Only the tearoom's straw mats (*tatami*) actually come from Japan.

This teahouse is named Kūan or Hut of Emptiness. It speaks to the Buddhist teaching that all things, including us, are empty. We and our experiences form in the complete emptiness of the moment before us, which arises from nothing and immediately vanishes. Since every moment of our life is without precedent and different than every other moment, every moment is unique.

Harbour View tells the same story. Like our lives, it arises from the people and families who find this place, fall in love with its beauties again and again, and so linger awhile, until they too give way to other people and other families.

Shenstones'

190 Harbour View Road

The Shenstone cottage is one of a small handful of properties at Harbour View that have been in the same family since first construction.

The earliest members of the family to discover the joys of summer on the Annapolis Basin were Joseph N. Shenstone (1855-1933) and his wife Eliza (1853-1926), along with their six children. The Shenstones lived in Toronto, where Joseph was a senior executive (and ultimately president) of Massey-Harris, the Canadian farm-equipment manufacturer later known as Massey Ferguson.

Joseph and Eliza's youngest child, Allen Goodrich Shenstone

(1893-1980), eventually became the cottage's long-time owner, before passing it on to his son Michael (1928-2019), in whose family it remains.

Allen, in an unfinished memoir from the late 1970s, provides an answer to the puzzling question of how this Toronto family with no Nova Scotia connections ended up creating a summer home in faraway Smith's Cove during the earliest years of the 20th century.

After explaining how the Cossaboom family transformed a farm house in Smith's Cove into an inn and summer resort in 1898, Allen writes: "The first person attracted to the place was a Mr. Lord, who had been summering at a nearby farm for a number of years. Mr. Lord was so taken by 'The Harbour View House'...that he leased a piece of land and built a private cabin on it. Our cousins, the Goodriches, were friends of the Lords and followed them to Harbour View, where they later on acquired one of the small log cottages. That resulted in attracting [our family] to join them in 1902 or 1903."

The Shenstones, then, were not the first—and would definitely not be the last—family to visit vacationing friends or relations at Harbour View and be so delighted by the place that they soon put down enduring summer roots of their own. (The Goodriches were a Massachusetts family that included Mrs. Kate Goodrich, the younger sister of Eliza Shenstone. According to Allen's notes on the 1931 Harbour View map, the Goodriches were early owners of the current Emberly cottage on Beachcomber Lane. The Mr. Lord mentioned is John B. Lord, whose sudden death during a Sunday dinner at the hotel is so memorably described in *The Harbour View Story*.)

During the Shenstones' first summers in Smith's Cove they took rooms at the hotel, and the spell was cast. "Mother soon became so enamoured of the beauty and comfort of the whole place," writes Allen, "that she never afterwards willingly went anywhere else for the summer."

He continues: "In 1907 Father leased a piece of land with waterfront and by 1908 a cabin had been built for us. It was planned by an architect and is much higher than any other cabin because he insisted on a steep roof. In fact, the sitting room [ceiling] was so high that a second floor was soon put in so that the fire would heat the room adequately."

Although the architect's name is lost to history, the builder was Ralph Cossitt, according to Charles Turnbull, who noted that this was Cossitt's first Harbour View project. He later went on to build other cottages and, most notably, St. Anne's Birch Chapel.

Initially the Shenstone cabin had no interior staircase and anyone sleeping on the newly-installed second floor (which, during the first generation, was the domain of the younger boys) had to scramble up a steep ladder from the ocean-side porch, then through a small door in the wall. A few years later, Ralph Cossitt built a proper staircase that rises from the living room, employing much the same birchbark style on the railing and banisters that he used to beautify the Birch Chapel.

Although the cottage at first glance appears to be built of logs, it is a conventional wood-frame structure but with external siding in the form of horizontal slabs of spruce and fir, with the bark still on it. Inside, the unusual defining feature of the living room is floor-to-ceiling panelling of rustic vertical slabs of spruce, again with the rough bark intact. Like many other Harbour View cottages, the room is anchored by a large stone fireplace.

Down through the generations, however, the primary living area during daylight hours has always been the long and exceptionally deep veranda overlooking the Basin.

Until about 1971, the Shenstones had their meals at the hotel, along with all the other Harbour View cottagers.

Allen's memoir notes that there were few automobiles in southwest Nova Scotia in the early years. Most summer visitors took the Dominion Atlantic trains to Smith's Cove from the ferry wharf in Digby, or from Yarmouth or Halifax. Once they were settled into Harbour View, transportation options were few: "Besides the railway, the only other means of transport were horse vehicles or sailboats, there being no motor boats. The quickest way to get to Digby if the wind was right was to sail and that is the way all the young went, but for the older folk a vehicle of some sort was necessary and vehicles could be rented with horse from the hotel. Our family usually had a surrey which we hired by the week. With a good horse it took about an hour to drive to Digby and at least two and a half hours to Annapolis."

Allen, as the youngest son, spent more of his childhood in Smith's Cove than his siblings, and bonded with the place deeply, and for life. Except for absences during both world wars, he spent almost every summer there, facilitated by the fact that he was a physics professor at Princeton University, with long summer breaks.

In a 1968 letter to the Irvines, soon after the they had bought the property, Allen wrote: "You do realize, I hope, how important Harbour View is to me. In many ways I feel more at home there than I do in Princeton where I have lived for 43 years. Perhaps my feelings come from my early youth before the First World War."

In 1947, Allen bought the Shenstone cottage from his step-mother's estate (his widowed father had remarried) and entered into a lease with Harbour View House and Cottages Ltd. for the lot beneath the cottage—like most of the other cottages at the time, the building was owned by the family but the land remained the property of Harbour View.

(It should be noted that Hester Bates, long-time owner of 142 Harbour View, was a granddaughter of Joseph and Eliza Shenstone, too, through her mother Nora, one of Allen's sisters. Fond child-hood memories of Harbour View brought Hester back as an adult. Her son Russell Fries was also a long-term summer resident in his own right.)

Allen had met his future wife, the London-born Molly Chadwick, in 1914 while studying at the University of Cambridge, and after they married in 1923 she too fell in love with Smith's Cove and the surrounding region, where she could often be found sitting at her easel, painting expert watercolours of the local vistas while Allen pursued his passion for sailing on the Annapolis Basin. Their son Michael was born in 1928 and, like his parents, spent summer va-cations whenever possible in Smith's Cove, and, like his father, was rarely happier than when sailing with his family.

Molly died in 1967, and Allen and Michael scattered her ashes on the waters of the Basin from Allen's beloved Lightning-class wooden sailboat, the *QE 2*.

The year 1969 brought two more major changes in the life of the cottage. Early in the year Allen completed negotiations to purchase the parcel of land beneath the building from David Irvine, with the deed registered in Michael's name.

And in August in the Birch Chapel, Allen remarried, to widow Tiffin Harper, who was a neighbour in Princeton, New Jersey.

The union of Allen and Tiffin led indirectly to an influx of new families to Harbour View—Tiffin's daughters Katherine Mead and Daisy Sharp (later Daisy Fitch) fell in love with the place and quickly put down roots of their own, soon shared by the younger generations.

Tiffin made a number of improvements to the cottage with an eye toward greater comfort and convenience, but in 1975 she and Allen relocated to the former Mathers cottage (now the Fitch cottage), thus passing full occupancy of 190 Harbour View to Michael, his wife Susan and their three children, Thomas, Barbara and Mary.

Michael's long career in the Canadian foreign service occasionally prevented the family from vacationing in Smith's Cove, but with his retirement in the early 1990s he and Susan were able to devote full summers to life at Harbour View, where they both did much to revive and expand the cottage's flower gardens, and especially their beloved old roses.

The 1980s and '90s also saw the arrival of grandchildren—Amy and Leith to Thomas and his then-wife Sally, and Sarah and Claire to Mary and her husband Christopher, becoming the fifth generation of Shenstones to savour vacations at Smith's Cove (with a sixth generation in the wings).

In recent years Thomas introduced his partner Brenda to Harbour View. And in the summer of 2016, many in the community gathered on the lawn below the cottage to witness the marriage of Barbara and Belinda.

Now, well into its second century, the Shenstone Cottage at Harbour View continues to be a much-cherished summer refuge for all the family.

Perryford

194 Harbour View Road

Let's begin this update of Perryford with a brief reprise from Charles H. Turnbull's excellent 1994 volume on Harbour View. The property was originally purchased from Bishop Jagger by Harry W. Ford, who sketched a design for the cottage, which was built in 1909, and named it Tuckaway. Ralph Cossitt finished the interior trim with yellow birch, cut in the winter so it retains its bark to this day, over a century later, similar to his work in the Birch Chapel nearby.

An avid gardener, Mr. Ford put in extensive gardens. For decades, the old piston pump often ran all day long in the summer to water them.

Upon Mr. Ford's death, his son, Webster H. Ford, inherited the property and lived there in the summers with his wife, Marjorie Olcott Ford. Upon his passing, Mrs. Ford put the property up for sale, and Rellen Flynn Perry bought it when visiting the area with her husband, Elmer V. Perry, Jr.

And now another historical thread. The Raymond family arrived at the Digby Basin from New Jersey sometime during the American Revolution. At one point in the 19th century they built clipper ships (Israel Raymond and Sons).

When that industry waned, one son, Newman H. Raymond, emigrated to Long Island, then New Jersey and finally northern Virginia, but he kept a large property in Bear River.

His daughter, Ruth Raymond, visited Bear River and environs frequently and brought her daughter Rellen (née Ruth Ellen Flynn), to visit in the summers.

Elmer and Rellen Perry married in 1943, while Captain Perry was serving during the war, so at the war's end they had a proper "honeymoon" and stayed at the Colonial Arms (since defunct) across the Bear River from Harbour View.

Returning with the whole family, they vacationed in Smith's Cove in 1962. The vacation ended with a vow to return the next year and look for a cottage. Hence, in 1963, Rellen bought the property from Marjorie Ford. As an acknowledgment of its heritage, she renamed the property Perryford.

Their son, Christopher, had the good fortune to come up for two whole summers beginning in 1964 and really bonded with the place. The property was never formally part of the Harbour View community, but the Perrys were welcomed by everyone, especially at Happy Hour or on walks after dinner.

Every summer, Rellen would stay about 12 weeks, and Elmer joined during his vacation. Upon his retirement, they both spent the whole summer there.

Christopher and his sister, Sheelagh Jean Perry, would visit, either together or at different times, over the years, but school, work and life's distractions limited these visits. Christopher missed a couple of years during medical school and residency.

He made up for the absence toward the end of medical school, twice spending several months shadowing Doctors Doug Lewis and Nuri Birsel, back when Digby General was a functioning hospital. That is the only time he delivered a baby (well, the woman did all the work). He loved going on home visits after dinner with Dr, Lewis, who knew everything about his patients!

Christopher recalls the pleasure of family lobster boils on the beach (he didn't get the "seafood lovers" gene, so roasted hot dogs), the pleasant relaxation and the frequent social gatherings.

What gorgeous weather summer can bring, and that one can appreciate while sitting on the veranda or outside, overlooking the beach.

Elmer majored in golf during the summers and Rellen majored in people, definitely not in gardening. Christopher came to relax, read, putter on the property, and enjoy everything. Among Christopher's "Harbour View Memories" is his mother, Rellen, befriending several school-age girls (e.g., Allison and Jane) and taking them to a proper tea.

Sadly, Sheelagh died in 1980 and Elmer in 1989, after which Christopher inherited his dad's share of Perryford.

Rellen and Christopher came to Harbour View every summer. Her last summer was touch and go. Despite undergoing chemotherapy, she was determined to visit. The thought of dying while at Perryford was less daunting than the idea of not going there at all!

In 1996, Christopher brought his soon-to-be wife, Antoinette, to visit over Canadian Thanksgiving, which happened to end with a furious storm. Fortunately she loved the property and, despite a ferry ride that left her convinced of imminent sinking, the passage didn't deter her from accepting his proposal! Of course, Rellen was relieved to hear that Antoinette loved Nova Scotia, too.

In recent decades, the Perrys made some updates to the property. They updated plumbing and electrical wiring, put in a new kitchen and shower, repaired the rip-rap at the base of the embankment, added a skylight to the cathedral living room ceiling and a deck outside the veranda. Sadly and suspiciously, during the skylight addition, three Maud Lewis paintings went missing. That legacy of Rellen's interactions with Maud was stolen.

So, what happened to all those beautiful gardens? The Perrys tried to keep them up for several years and then gave in to reality and gradually scaled them way back. The trellised roses remain, however, as do the gorgeous views of the Basin from the veranda and deck.

In 2005, Christopher and Antionette had their newborn daughter, Christiana, baptized at the Birch Chapel. Afterward, a wonderful party down at the house with many of Rellen and Elmer's friends showcased the future legacy of Perryford.

Christiana has enjoyed the property most when she brought a friend (Rosemary), and her father had the pleasure of photos of neighborhood water fights, and, another time, the two of them actually winning his $5 bet that they wouldn't swim in the basin. He had won a similar 25-cent bet (a witness to inflation!) from his mother in 1964 with a quick, full dunk, but ran out screaming. Christiana and Rosemary actually swam for awhile!

As of this writing, Christopher has largely retired from his academic position as Professor of Psychiatry at McGill University and now leads a less-traveled life. Antoinette and Christiana make it to Perryford with him, depending on schedules and health issues.

He continues his psychiatric practice at Pittsfield, Massachusetts, where he and Antoinette live. Health permitting, they look to spend more time at Perryford over the ensuing decades, as it is a little piece of heaven.

Pillikan

208 Harbour View Road

The story of 208 Harbour View Road is closely linked to a chance encounter in Vienna, Austria in the 1980s.

The late Michael Shenstone was in those days the Canadian ambassador to Austria. There he met Beowulf Klebert (Beo) and they became very good friends. One summer, Michael invited Beo to join him and his family at their cottage in Harbour View.

Beo did indeed visit his dear friend and, as the story goes, one afternoon, after a nice lunch and pleasant conversation, he fell asleep on the daybed on the veranda at the Shenstone house. As he woke up, looking out at the sea, he immediately fell in love with the view and the atmosphere. Beo was then looking for a house in this area, preferably close to his friends. First he bought a piece of land and considered building a house there. Luckily enough, shortly after, the house on 208 Harbour View Road, which had belonged to the Prescesky family, became available and Beo bought it. He gave the cottage the Mi'kmaq name Pilllikan, which means "house by the water".

Beo renovated the house completely and had major changes done in the inside, including a heating system that made the house also fit for the winter. He had the smaller additional building re-modelled with a bedroom and bathroom upstairs and planned to later convert the original garage into an additional living room and kitchen. He had the garage moved to the main house with a living room on top.

Before this sunroom, which is the expert craftsmanship of Percy Potter, was completed, Beo sadly passed away in 2007.

New windows in the enclosed veranda, which has a fantastic view of Digby Gut.

Beo made several fantastic friends in the Harbour View com-munity and the area. He really appreciated the immense friendli-ness and hospitality of the people, enjoyed the seafood and the peace and quiet.

His two sons, Philipp and Sebastian, inherited the house. They have very fond memories of many vacations spent there with their father. Together with their mother, Brigitta, they continue to make the long trip from Vienna, Austria, which is their home, to spend part of their summers at the house, enjoying the special atmosphere of Harbour View and exploring the area, the beautiful landscape and the many historic sites.

Adirondack / Muskoka chairs built by Percy Potter

Westerly

234 Harbour View Road

The cottage at the end of the road was originally constructed by Russell Fries and his first wife, Sylvia, in 1972. It was built on land that Russell had purchased from Walter Flett in 1967, a year of major transition for Harbour View as it was the same year that Walter Flett sold the Harbour View House and Cottages to Sylvia and Dave Irvine. After the wooded lot was cleared, the cottage was constructed under the supervision of Allen Moore's father.

The cottage was unlike most of the cottages at Harbour View for a couple of reasons, most notably because it was untraditional in design. Second, while it had cedar-shingled siding, the siding was originally stained red. Surrounded by birch trees and grass lawn, the place had a serenity and privacy which Russell cherished year in and year out.

165

Russell and his second wife, Ann, decided in 2004 to expand the cottage by adding an extra bedroom and loft space, and by enclosing part of the water-side deck to make a sunroom. They also decided to stain the cottage gray, as it has remained to this day. It was here, particularly in their new sunroom, that Russell and Ann hosted many a cocktail gathering with visitors relishing not only the conviviality of the occasion but the views to the north and west, with the Digby Gut as the centrepiece.

The history of the cottage would be incomplete without honouring both Russell and Ann, who loved the cottage dearly just as they loved Harbour View, the place where they met many years before. Ann passed away in November, 2017, after successfully holding cancer at bay for 13 years. Russell tragically passed away in August 2022 while riding his bicycle along the Landsdowne Road between Smiths Cove and Bear River. Their memory lingers...as does their vision for life on the Point.

Upon Russell's passing, it was infeasible for either of his two children to take on the cottage, as they lived abroad, Tom in Norway and Gwyneth in Singapore. Fortuitously, the cottage had certain aspects akin to a traditional house and was partially winterized, meaning that the season at Harbour View could be extended —by a lot. Accordingly, David and Suzie Turnbull purchased it in 2023 for use by family and friends, not only in the summer but during the extended seasons.

That the cottage was purchased by a Turnbull represents a certain circularity. The centre of the viewshed is the point of land where the first Turnbulls settled in Canada after taking passage from Scotland in 1786. William Turnbull and his family were the first settlers of what was then known as 'Bay View', several miles from the town of Digby on the west side of the Digby Gut. Their first house, near the corner where the Lighthouse Road joins the Shore Road, still stands, albeit having been much modified from the log cabin it had originally been. Living in what was a dense forest, the only way for these early settlers to get to Digby was by walking along the shore to town.

One of William's great-grandsons, William Wallace Turnbull, lived in Bear River with his family. After his father's early death he moved across the Bay of Fundy to Saint John, New Brunswick to find a job that would enable him to support his mother and eight siblings back in Bear River, who lived in a now-abandoned house that still stands along the main street.

In time, the family moved to Saint John and nearby Rothesay, where his grandson, also named William Wallace Turnbull, (David's grandfather), was born and raised, and where many Turnbull relatives live still.

The spirit of those ancestors who first inhabited these shores some two and a half centuries ago serves not only to connect their descendants to a shared family history but attaches them to the Annapolis Basin that has provided a long-standing place of 'home.'

Since the cottage had no known name when it was purchased, the Turnbulls decided to give it a name in keeping with the local tradition. The name 'Westerly' evokes not only the cottage's outlook, but the direction of the prevailing breeze.

David Irvine's 'Argonaut' standing tall in the mud flats at low tide, 1968

The Cottagers' Association

The Association takes a group portrait at the pool party each year

The Harbourview Cottagers Association

The Harbourview Cottagers Association was created in 1988 in response to the Irvines' decision to sell the land that held the playground, tennis court and swimming pool, and his suggestion that the cottagers assume ownership of those assets.

To achieve this, six cottage owners (Christopher Hopgood, Charles Turnbull, James MacLean, Cathy Boyle, Wendy Emberly and John Carling) set up a non-profit corporation with a board of directors, and sold shares in the Association for $1,000 per cottage to raise money to purchase and support the facilities the new Association would own.

In 1991, the Association installed new playground equipment. In 1992 the old, run-down tennis court was replaced with a new one, which saw many years of annual tennis tournaments. The court has been resurfaced several times since, and in 2022 pickleball lines were added, extending to the symphony of sounds that come from the entire recreation area.

The Association also purchased the water system, the pump house and the road system, all vital to the community. These were sold by Mona and Phil Webb, who were owners of the Harbourview Inn at the time, and who had purchased the road and water systems from Mona's brother, David Irvine. The Webbs wanted to turn those assets over to the Association, and completed the sale in 1996. The old lead piping in the water system was eventually upgraded to PVC piping.

In 2016, the cottagers voted to replace the old concrete swimming pool with a new, vinyl-lined pool. This was made possible by the far-sighted establishment of a capital fund some years before for this very purpose. That fund had grown substantially by the time it was obvious that the old pool needed to be replaced, but it wasn't enough to cover the $168,000 price tag from R & R Pools. To cover the balance, five cottage owners (Cliff Langin, Mike Emberly, Jim Mountain, Lee Harwood and Harold Clapp) generously volunteered to enter into a private, five-year loan agreement with the Association for the additional $60,000 needed. That loan was paid off in full in 2021.

Chris Hopgood and Mike Emberly at the annual pool party

When cottagers arrived in the summer of 2017, they found a gorgeous new pool in place of the grassy spot that had once adjoined the old pool. They also saw that the steps were moved to the south end and the diving board to the north end of the pool. There was also a new pool house, and wide concrete decking all around the pool made room for many more chairs than before. Chain link fence replaced the wooden fence along the water side of the pool and the new grassy area, meaning there was now a wide-open view to the Basin.

The most recent addition to pool area was a changing room

built onto the side of the pool house in 2023.

In addition to the pool and the tennis court, the kids' playground has also seen a lot of action over the years on the equipment and on the lawn. The original equipment was replaced in 1996, and updated equipment was installed in 2024.

Since the establishment of the Association, the pool area has been the site of the annual Pool Party, which is always held on the Sunday of the August long weekend, after the annual general meeting on Saturday. Generations of children now have happy memories of the kids' games in the pool and on the grass, as well as of the dessert table at the annual picnic! The collection of pool party photos in the Langins' barn is a vivid demonstration of the explosion of kids and families and guests who have enjoyed this Harbour View tradition over the years.

The Association is strong because of the cottagers who have volunteered their time to serve as Directors on the Executive Board, and thanks to those who have stepped up to lead as President over the years, including Cliff Langin, Mike Emberly, Chris Hopgood, Russell Boyle, Doug Irvine and Suzie Turnbull. At this writing, Mike Emberly is at the helm, returning to the role he took on in the early years of the Association.

One of the best decisions that the Association made in 2000 was to approach Kevin McCully to maintain the grounds and various facilities from early spring of each year to season closing after Thanksgiving weekend. Kevin and his wife, Shaunda, have become part of the Harbour View family throughout the years, having shown their commitment to all the cottagers to ensure that the facilities are maintained. The cottagers are well blessed with Kevin and Shaunda. Let's hope they stay as long as possible.

It should be noted, that as of this writing, all purchases have been paid for and the Association has a very healthy cash balance, with money in reserve in case of emergencies. Annual dues increases have stayed well below the inflation rate since the Association's inception in 1988. Credit goes to all the cottagers and their board of directors for their forward-looking approach to help make Harbour View what it is today.

Joan Carling

Memorial

Award

LAST OUT!
Harbourview

Certificate awarded to the last swimmer out of the pool each season.

Harbour View Mud Pie

One 8-ounce package of
chocolate wafers
1/2 cup butter
1 1/2 pounds coffee ice
cream, softened
1/3 cup cocoa (Cadburys)

3 tablespoons butter
2/3 cup + 2 tablespoons sugar
1 1/3 cup whipping cream
2 teaspoons vanilla extract
Two squares semi-sweet
chocolate for garnish

Early in the day –
- Pre-heat oven to 375°
- Crush chocolate wafers into crumbs.
- In small saucepan over low heat, melt 1/2 cup butter.
- Combine crumbs and butter in 9-inch pie plate and press mixture to bottom and side of plate.
- Bake at 375° for 10 minutes—NO LONGER. Cool crust completely on wire rack.
- Carefully spread softened ice cream into crust.

Freeze until firm, about one and a half to two hours.

When the pie is frozen –
- In large saucepan, combine cocoa, 2/3 cup sugar, 1/3 cup of whipping cream, and 3 tablespoons butter
- Cook at low heat until mixture is smooth and about to boil.
- Remove from heat and stir in 1 teaspoon vanilla.
- Remove pie from freezer.
- Cool mixture slightly, then pour over coffee ice cream.
- Return pie to freezer for at least one hour, or a day ahead.

Serving

- *Important*: Take pie out of freezer about a half hour before serving.
- Whip cream and add sugar and 1 teaspoon vanilla, and spread over pie.
- Make chocolate curls if you wish.
- Serve!

Bon appétit
Mona Webb